POSTADOLESCENCE

THEORETICAL AND CLINICAL ASPECTS
OF PSYCHOANALYTIC THERAPY

Rudolph Wittenberg

GRUNE & STRATTON   New York and London

This is a volume in a series under the consultant editorship
of Leopold Bellak.

Contents

Introduction

THIS BOOK is intended for clinicians who work analytically—mainly through exploration, rather than suggestion—with young adults from their late teens to their early twenties. It is divided into a theoretic and a clinical part. The first, theoretic part consists of a presentation of both the metapsychologic and socioeconomic factors that characterize post adolescence. The clinical, second part of the book is the application of theory to practice.

In writing this book I am making the assumption that post adolescence is not delayed adolescence, nor do I see the characteristic problems of young adulthood as failures in the adolescent struggle. Instead, I am suggesting that postadolescence represents a specific phase of growth in the life cycle.

Differentiations in ego states throughout the growth cycle—between infancy and early childhood, latency and adolescence—have been made in both theoretic and clinical writing, particularly in the past twenty years since Anna Freud's formulation that in puberty the ego alienates itself from the superego, with all this statement implies. The onset and middle phase of adolescence have been described, but there is less material on the end-phase of adolescence and the period of transition leading to adulthood. Indeed, one may ask, just what constitutes the end of adolescence?

Spiegel suggested that "adolescence ends when the individual finds a non-incestuous love-object, and tender as well as sexual drives are directed toward this same object with the goal of sexual gratification, i.e., when sexuality is fully integrated into the personality."[1]

That this definition concentrates on the drive cathexis without a central recognition of the ego is understandable if we recognize that we have moved since the fifties from the topographic to the structural theory in psychoanalysis, and with it may now be in a better position to approach the definition of termination of adolescence and the subsequent period.

iv

Basically, the structural theory emphasizes the genetic or developmental aspect of mental functioning, while the topographic theory, as Freud had anticipated, "did not offer an adequate explanation of mental functioning."[2]

When Arlow and Brenner in the above-quoted work paraphrase the famous dictum: "Where id was there shall ego be" to read: "Where super-ego was there shall be ego," one is reminded of the difference in ego states in adolescent patients who had returned a few years later, either during a crisis in college or graduate school. "When I graduated from high school," one young woman recalls "I felt that there was nothing I *had* to do. Everything was now up to me. And this is when real trouble started."

The "real trouble" is the ego in postadolescence which can be defined by five *metapsychologic characteristics:* the self-image crisis—a sharp vascillation between superego and ego-ideals; certain aspects of the identity diffusion—brief states of depersonalization as well as acting out of psychosexual conflicts through substitute solutions; the necessity of giving up all adolescent role-playing; the necessity to cope fully with time-continuity; the choice of the partner, which is often bypassed by an escape into unsuccessful marriages.

These five metapsychologic characteristics comprise the following chapters of the first section.

This is followed by Socioeconomic Factors, which further characterize postadolescence: the economic bind, which consists of young adults' needs to be self-supporting while society is keeping them out of the marketplace, but profits from them as consumers; group-formation and social isolation, the specific function of groups at this phase of growth as distinguished from adolescent groups, the relationship to fluctuating ego states; the quest for a *Weltanschauung,* which comprises the complex integration of both psychologic and sociologic aspects of postadolescence.

After the discussion of both metapsychologic and socioeconomic characteristics of postadolescence, an attempt has been made in Part II to spell out in detail the clinical implications of the theoretic considerations. Beginning with the specific problems of the referral triangle due to the partial economic dependency of young adults, the initial consultation is discussed with adaptations of the standard analytic interview model to postadolescent patients. The core of this part consists of considerations of variations in technique, as distinguished from modifications and applied to such key issues as transference and countertransference, styles of free associations, aspects of intervention and interpretation, some special technical problems, and a last chapter on education for analysis, for the minority of young adults who can afford—in every sense—a complete classical psychoanalysis.

Among the kind friends and colleagues who have made constructive suggestions for changes are Dr. Leopold Bellak, who launched the venture, Sandra Bemesderfer, Dr. Milton Kapit and particularly Dr. Henry and Dr. Yella Lowenfeld, with their discussions about the self-image, countertransference and other clinical aspects throughout the manuscript. To them and others, as well as to the authors whose work I have quoted goes my sincere appreciation.

PART I: Postadolescence as a Specific Phase of Growth

METAPSYCHOLOGIC CHARACTERISTICS

1. The Self-Image Crisis

WHILE ADOLESCENCE is characterized by the alienation of the superego from the ego, as Anna Freud suggested, the task of the ego in post-adolescence is to achieve a workable compromise between the superego and differing ego-ideals. This task is complicated by considerable fluctuation, due to degrees of superego investment and withdrawal in one ego-ideal or another. At times this process seems like a dilemma, a choice between equally undesirable alternatives; for other periods it appears as a predicament or a quandry, but it does remain a matter of considerable conflict throughout the entire postadolescent phase. This aspect of young adulthood represents the end of a prolonged struggle for an equilibrium and reaches a critical stage only now, when binding choices and far reaching decisions are expected. The complexity of the struggle, together with the inner and outer pressures at this time of the growth cycle combine to make this one of the metapsychological characteristics of postadolescence. It may be called: Self-Image Crisis.

While the self-image—unlike the identity struggle—has its roots at the end of the oedipal period, it is a more encompassing development, involving not only id, ego and superego, but the body and its parts. As Hartmann suggested, the concept "self refers to the whole person of an individual, including his body and psychic organization."[3]

Historically, the concept of the superego and the ego-ideal did not only go through a number of changes during Freud's lifetime—from considering the two identical to a definite separation—but interpretations vary to this day.

McLaughlin, as well as Erikson, among others delimit the superego from the ego-ideal, while Jacobson does not think it possible to separate "the ego-ideal from the morally prohibitive . . . super-ego, since they undeniably represent a functional unit . . ."[4]

The alienation of the superego from the ego during adolescence suggests that a separation exists between the two systems, since the ego-ideals in adolescence are not necessarily affected by the superego alienation. It is precisely because the superego makes powerful and insistent claims in postadolescence, thus forcing the conflict with ego-ideals into the open, that we have the self-image quandary.

The ego during postadolescence is usually not strong enough to balance the conflicting demands of superego and ego-ideals, making for a distressing instability in behavior of which the young adult is well aware, without always being able to control it. Characteristically during the middle of the adolescent period, young people cope with the dilemma in one of two ways. They may line up ego-ideal and superego in a straight row, hoping to avoid the dilemma by doing things "because of" authority, family, church and school. They walk the "straight and narrow" which is the line that is meant to avoid the conflict; they are "good"—model students, regular church attendants, helpful to family and community.

The other possibility of avoiding the dilemma is by taking the opposite direction. They turn their back on the superego and act out the ego-ideal demands, by doing things "in spite of" authority, family, society.

In other words, the adolescent has avoided the full impact of the self-image predicament by taking a polarized opposition-conformity position which was a substitute for autonomy. He would either agree or disagree with some authority and thereby never have to struggle toward an independent stand.

Now comes the time when it dawns on the late adolescent that there are fewer and fewer authorities with whom to agree or disagree, that he is rapidly becoming his own authority. As one young adult put it: "The idea that there are no rule books is rather frightening." From the recognition of this new state—an expectation of autonomy—to the full mastery comprises the whole phase of postadolescence. Frequently, the ego fails in mediating the conflict between ego-ideal and superego during this phase of the growth cycle.

For the therapist who observes the unfolding of this self-image dilemma in his postadolescent patients, it is important diagnostically to differentiate between a true ego-ideal and a pseudoideal which sometimes is an expression of grandiose, megalomanic strivings which "have either survived unchecked since childhood or became revived and so much intensified in adolescence that they have succeeded in entering and asserting themselves enduringly in the superego and the goals of the ego under the guise of an ideal."[4]

One will find this constellation in a number of young adults who suffered from serious learning disturbances in the second and third year of college. Instead of struggling with a balance between their ego-ideal and their superego, these young people had failed to develop a true ego-ideal in the first place and were left with the impossible task of trying to reach a balance between a pseudo-ideal and a harsh superego. It took the form of believing—as they had always been led to assume—

that they were "a genius," superior to the mundane requirements of a college and the acquisition of facts and knowledge. While their good intelligence and charm had been enough to get them through high school (although during the last year they had already experienced difficulties) it is in postadolescence, during the first or second year of college, that they find themselves totally unable to invest libido in their studies. Their pseudoideal demands that they not "give in" to requirements meant for the "average man," while their superego clearly pressures the ego to face the tasks ahead and cope with assignments, tests, and marks.

Often the young adult cannot find any resolution to this conflict and needs help. The self-image dilemma has gone beyond the more usual distress patterns and become pathologic.

While we have left the clinical implications of this state for the second part of the book, it may be helpful to point out even in this theoretic discussion that the therapy of the self-image conflicts presents particular difficulties, because we often find ourselves supporting the superego, which had too much power in the first place. This development comes about through our failure to first clarify the confusion in the ego-ideal before we move to reality testing, which is inevitably taken as an appeal to the superego. A therapist may say something like this: "Perhaps you are an unusually brilliant young man, but without hard work all your potential ability won't get you very far." The patient assumes that we have taken his pseudoideal as his real ego-ideal and just want him to work a little harder. Actually, all we have succeeded in doing is to make the superego more demanding, keep the pseudoideal intact, and prevent any further resolution of the self-image dilemma which should result in a flexible, functioning ego. With this statement the patient cannot build his ego to the point where it can provide him with enough pleasure in working. He may, at best, work in spite of himself, derive no ego-syntonic gratifications, and cling to his unrealistic pseudoideal which further prevents him from realistic pleasure.

Perhaps the best way to make the distinction between real and pseudo ego-ideal is to recall Freud's formulation: "That which he projects ahead of him as his ideal is merely his substitute for the lost narcissism of his childhood—the time when he was his own ideal."[5] Freud goes from here to the important relationship between the forming of ideals and sublimation and emphasizes that the "narcissism that now seems to be displaced on this new ideal ego . . . deems itself the possessor of all perfections." To the extent to which the ego-ideal has remained a representative of the primary omnipotent fantasies, it is the pseudoideal in postadolescence, not one that is anchored in reality.

If we recall that the ego-ideal has also a "social side" as Freud pointed out in this same paper on Narcissism, we get another dimension of this concept, which "has great importance for the understanding of group psychology." When Freud says that the ego-ideal is "also the common ideal of a family, a class or a nation," he points to the sociopsychologic factors which will be discussed in a separate part.

Throughout the whole of postadolescence the ego is struggling toward a persistent position, that is as independent from previous influences as possible. Society now demands that the young adult take a stand, declare who he really is, what his convictions are, whom he loves and whom he hates.

That he has real difficulties in reaching a conflict-free state is often seen in the way in which young people feel about being in therapy. Of course, a young adult's hesitation to admit being in therapy has much to do with the transference, but more specifically, it is related to the self-image dilemma. Where he has the pseudoideal, he cannot bear the idea of being "imperfect," of having enough problems to require clinical intervention. He will not want anybody to know about his being in treatment, even though he may have many good feelings about his analyst at the time. Opposed to this pseudoideal is his superego which insists that he be honest with close friends and not resort to subterfuge every time he has an analytic appointment. He may say: "I should tell my girl friend about coming here, she would understand it, in fact she has wondered about some positive changes in my behavior—but I don't want her to know that I need help, that I can't function without you, the therapist." This is another illustration of the self-image dilemma in a case where the superego pushes the pseudoideal.

For an illustration of the self-image quandary with conflicting ego-ideals we may take the young adult who is deeply involved in his chosen art or profession—evolved via sublimation as his ego-ideal—and whose wife presents him with a baby, a situation which drastically alters his style of life, his limited income, his free time with his wife. One of his ego-ideals—supported by the superego—will demand that he live up to its side: to be a good father, a good husband, a decent human being. Another ego-ideal will make its claims: the whole-hearted dedication to his work which he considers his whole life. If he feels resentful about taking time or money away from his work for the child and family, he will hear from his superego, contained in the other ideal: You are a selfish, small little man. If he appeases the superego and does "the right thing," one of his ego-ideals will object: Why are you stopping your painting, your research to take care of the baby for the afternoon? Is this how you hope to achieve your ends?

Conflicting ego-ideals versus the superego—this is what is meant by a self-image predicament.

This should not be confused with "ambivalence" which requires the simultaneous existence of the impulse to preserve and to destroy the object. It would be important in therapy to distinguish clearly between the self-image conflicts and a state of ambivalence toward love objects. Both may exist in one patient, but a differential diagnosis would determine whether we focus on the self-image quandary or the ambivalence. The differentiating factor would probably be found in a careful investigation of the history: If ambivalence is the prominent aspect, it would most likely have shown up in many or even all significant relationships in the patient's past; if it appears to be a more recent manifestation, it would seem likely that one is dealing not so much with real ambivalence but the postadolescent self-image dilemma. Clearly, this differentiation would chart two very different therapeutic courses.

Another significant distinction in post adolescence can be made by observing the specific ways in which the young adult attempts to cope with the ever-present self-image predicament: to which aspect of his conflicts he gives the greater weight. Young people may direct most or all of their energies toward the different ego-ideals. Such shifting of superego weight would give the illusion of being without conflict, of having solved the self-image dilemma. In order to make this "solution" seem as real as possible, the postadolescent will often be intense or fervent in his support of one or the other of the conflicting aspects.

The young man may support one ego-ideal or his pseudo-ideal, or he may tend toward another, or he may vascillate between the two states rapidly, causing himself acute anxiety. An example of the rapid vascillation will be seen in the discussion of a young woman whose case we shall cover more fully in the following chapter. For a time her pseudo-ideal demanded that she live the life of a "true lesbian." When she found this demand too painful, she attempted to live up to the superego demand, by becoming a conventional bride and wife in a socially accepted marriage. This state became so intolerable to the fractured ego that she found herself unable to function without therapy.

Another way in which the vascillation between different ego-ideals and superego may appear could be seen in the case of a young college student who had formed one ego-ideal of a maverick, an unconventional, "different" kind of writer and scholar. In this capacity he wanted to be bracketed with a certain crowd on campus, known as the "cool" guys who disobeyed rules and protested on principle anything that represented status quo. At other times he found himself acutely uncomfortable with this identification, because it did not represent his other ideal: to be a conscientious student who gets very high marks and makes the dean's list, writes honor papers, and is considered a serious scholar by the serious group of students in his department.

When this young man felt loyal to one ego-ideal, he denounced the "bookish, square guys," stayed up late into the night, working on avant-garde "abstract" plays with one of the "way-out" groups on campus. At other periods, when the other ideal was in control, he worked feverishly, hiding his high marks from the avant-garde crowd, making excuses for his absences from their meetings, rather than admit that he had been studying.

This last illustration highlights still another aspect of the self-image conflicts: the importance of the self-representation, the way in which one wants to be seen or regarded by the significant people or groups in the environment, the so-called "reference group." There may be several different reference groups (the "cool" guys and the "serious" students), but more often in postadolescence young people attempt to pattern themselves after the reference group that represents the ego-ideal. This is what Freud referred to when he spoke of the "ego-ideal" as the "common ideal of a family, class or nation."[5]

While the process of locating the ideal reference group originally had involved the superego, by the time young people are lined up with their club or organization, their political or religious cause, the group represents the collective personification of the individual's ego-ideal. This is much more characteristic for postadolescence than for earlier phases of the adolescent development. For this reason the clinician needs to pay particular attention to the young adult's choice of reference groups, because nothing will give him a more accurate picture of his patient's ego-ideal than the structure, purpose, and interaction of his reference group. This is not the same as the identification with earlier groups, such as Scouts or interest groups, because these still involve the superego to a much larger degree than in postadolescence. They were the groups that home or school highly approved of, and to belong to them represented a superego representation. It follows that when the superego alienates itself from the ego—at the height of adolescence—young people gradually leave these groups, a fact that is substantiated by the dropout studies of most young peoples' groups.

The postadolescent reference group is more stable, as long as it can fulfill ego-ideal requirements which the young adult has projected on to them. When the ideal reference group is threatened by superego representatives—such as government or school authorities—the young adult experiences acute conflict, which is the expression of the self-image dilemma that had been dormant, while his reference group seemed stable and reliable. Young people will attempt to avoid this unpleasant state by a defensive position, by direct aggression against the critics of the reference group, or by abandoning one former ego-ideal group and joining with the representatives who have brought about the conflict. (This is of course a variation of the original defense mechanism, which Anna Freud had called identifying with the agressor.)

In time, young people may succeed in striking a balance between the ego-ideals, with the ego in full control. Only when different state has been reached can we consider the self-image conflicts resolved. In postadolescence where the ego is assailed by this and other conflicts which we shall discuss in the following chapters, the ego is usually not in the best position to reach this reasonable compromise. What complicates the struggle is the attitude of authority representatives which more often than not tends to strengthen the superego forces. When the young adult, after his college president's attack against his reference group, turns his back on the controversial organization and joins the adult critics, he is being rewarded by his elders with the dubious assurance: "I'm glad you are leaving the rebels and seeing the light." From the viewpoint of the adult authority this position is perfectly understandable. However, viewed clinically, the young adult has not solved his self-image predicament nor strengthened the hard-pressed ego. He feels that he has deserted his friends and is a "regular part of the establishment." He is not any more at peace with this solution than he had been when his reference group had been under attack. If the superego is punitive and harsh, the choice may help his standing in school, but it will also have made a future ego integration more difficult.

An attack against the reference group which represents one ego-ideal may also drive the postadolescent to a more determined clinging to this group, crystallize his position as a permanent member of the group or the ideas it stands for. Particularly in young people who have not fully resolved their oedipal conflicts—and who therefore would tend to avoid reliance on the still alienated superego—the forces that represent this ego-ideal will be felt as ego-syntonic and often become necessary for their emotional balance. The many young people who leave the cultural, political or religious affiliations of their family frequently have taken these opposing roads because the self-image quandary forced them to make a premature choice. Historical and current examples are too well known to require repetition, but in most situations where a young man of one faith chooses a different religion, where a young woman of a pronounced liberal political family selects the most conservative affiliation, they will say that they made their choices based on what was "right for me," instead of "what I should do."

This should not be misconstrued to read that young people who choose opposites from their families in basic issues are doing so only because they have not resolved the "oedipal conflict." This oversimplification does justice neither to the interpreter nor the young people. The same faulty argument may be made for young adults who follow very closely in the footsteps of their families "because their superego had been too powerful, due to insufficient resolution of the oedipal conflict, leading to an identification with the aggressor."

In both cases we miss the point, which is that the self-image quandary is forcing many young people to rely too heavily on one or the other of the conflicting ego-ideals. We should certainly remain aware of the fact that the difference between pathology and health is a matter of degree and that a great many young people during postadolescence vascillate from reliance on one ego-ideal to another, with varying superego investments, without a firm or permanent libidinal commitment to either group. A certain amount of moderation and yielding in this battle should be considered normal for postadolescence with the result that many young people change reference groups and with it, attitudes and opinions without making necessarily long-range choices. In the process of resolving the self-image dilemma, which does not require therapy in the lives of all young people, the ego balance is gradually accomplished, and with it, long-range choices are made with caution and based on mature thinking and reflection.

We should remain aware of the fact that while the self-image conflicts are one of the characteristics of postadolescence, they are not necessarily resolved in post adolescence. We know from our own analysis, from our patients and social contacts, that a great many adults have not succeeded in truly resolving this dilemma, although they may have established a relatively stable compromise.

2. Aspects of Identity Diffusion

THE UNEVEN PACE of ego integration and drive organization gives the struggle for identity a particular aspect during postadolescence. Definitions of "identity" vary in the literature quite as widely as the interpretations of "self-image." Indeed, they range from the synthetic to the ontogenetic, from socio psychologic statements to metapsychologic formulations.

Although one notices that most authors begin with the close connection between identification and identity, they come out with widely differing definitions. To establish a framework, I am referring on one side to Erikson who states that "identity formation . . . begins where the usefulness of identification ends"[6]—and on the other end to Jacobson who prefers to understand "identity formation as a process that builds up the ability to preserve the whole psychic organization as a highly individualized but coherent entity which has direction and continuity *at any stage of human development* (italics mine)."[7] In other words, you have on one side a sociologically weighted orientation with the resulting emphasis on puberty and beyond as highly significant for identity formation, and on the other end a strict metapsychologic orientation with the major emphasis on the infantile development, the deep roots of the original subject-object symbiosis, the drive theory, and the fusions between self and object images.

Within this framework one can find a great number of authors on both sides. On the sociopsychologic side we have Wheelis[8] or Lynd,[9] who leans heavily on Sullivan when he suggests that the "sense of identity is disturbed when a person cannot find aspects in his social situation with which he can clearly identify." Erikson states this even more definitively when he connects identity with the "maintenance of an inner solidarity with a group's ideals."[6]

The metapsychologic formulations by such authors as Mahler[10] or Greenacre,[11] who are close to Jacobson, see the sense of a feeling of identity in connection with the constitution of bodily and mental self-images of the child.[7]

The main difference between the two camps is in the emphasis on the role of the ego in infancy and, again, in adolescence.

The difficulty in defining identity may be eased by considering the British theoretician Edward Glover, who considers the preoccupation with identity a "modern obsession" and questions the use of the concept altogether.[12] He doubts that one can "deal in structural terms with a specific compound of ego feeling." In a challenging paper, called "Metapsychology or Metaphysics," Glover doubts that such terms as "identity diffusion" mean anything or that "they comprise the whole of psychoanalytic psychology: the influence of instincts, the development of the ego and of object relationships, the part played by a sequence of mental mechanisms and, finally, constitutional and environmental factors." He contrasts the vastness of the aspects implied in the term with the concept of the ego and suggests that "the concept of the ego has never arrogated to itself such a profusion of interrelated factors." He says that "no term that involves such a complicated interaction of factors and phases of development can lay claim to the status of basic mental concepts."

In returning to the dictionary for a nonpsychoanalytic but "crisp, if circumscribed definition," he suggests a "persisting quality of the experience of sameness."

For a discussion of the characteristics of postadolescence this limited definition of identity is useful because it makes it possible to focus on ego states and ego boundaries, both of which are particularly helpful concepts for the understanding of this phase of development.

When discussing identity in this book I am referring to the concept as a struggle toward a persistent experience of sameness, a process of the ego that emerged out of the earliest attempts toward autonomy, toward separation from the original symbiotic state and incestuous objects.

In defining the struggle for identity as an ego function, one can think of the conflict and the diffusion at every phase of development.

In the early twenties we expect a relatively stable drive organization, an acceptable mode of coping with drive cathexis, a more or less permanent resolution of bisexual conflicts. The ego of the young adult has not quite caught up with this development, as it were, so that one gets the impression at times that he functions in spite of himself. We could speak more of self-representation than an identity. This is what is meant by the uneven pace of ego integration and drive organization.

The other factor that makes the struggle for an identity more acute in postadolescence than before and after is the sudden change from the same familiar environment to a more impersonal, detached state. These environmental changes, which we will discuss more fully in the second half of Part I, should be noted here as one of the contributing factors that often provoke the identity crisis that has been avoided to some degree until now. The concept: changed environment implies more than the replacement of the comfortable room at home to the dormitory or army camps; it includes the contact with new cultures and modes of living, the change in the community, living habits, the contact with often impersonal authorities—to mention but the most obvious factors implied in the term "changed environment."

Both the changed environment and the uneven pace of drive organization and ego integration may produce the postadolescent identity crisis which, when unrelieved, may lead to a number of symptoms of which brief states of depersonalization seem to be one of the more characteristic ones.

Depersonalization has many aspects and occurs in neurotic as well as borderline states; however, several authors have reported that brief experiences of depersonalization can be observed in normal persons.[13] It is related to an absence of the familiar feeling of sameness, primarily within the personality, but also when the environment rapidly changes, as after quick flights into unknown countries without the chance to settle in any one. However, the significant aspect of depersonalization was pointed out by Federn,[14] who emphasized that it arises from a disturbance in a person's relation with his own self. The Psychiatric Dictionary defines it as "the process . . . of losing the identity . . ."[15]

A young woman in her early twenties reported states of depersonalization during her analysis when she experienced parts of her body as not belonging to her or sensing the feet much further removed from the top of the body than she knew they were. This young woman had sat up, facing me for a period prior to analysis on the couch, and recalled that once when I addressed her and used the word "you," her impulse had been to turn around to see to whom I had been talking. The patient was describing one of many different states of self representation in conflict with each other.

The existence of a number of such separate states makes it difficult for the young adult to achieve the feeling of a persistent experience of sameness. The "playing dead" aspect of depersonalization is frequently counteracted by artificial elation and the use of hallucogenic drugs.

Characteristically, the drugs are taken most often in groups, where the presence of other young people not only provides the comfort of group contagion but counteracts feelings of depersonalization.

One young college student reported a brief state of depersonalization at the start of his freshman year, when he was several thousand miles from home.

"I was standing in my room, looking over the empty parking lot outside my window. It was snowing, and there weren't any people. I didn't want to study anymore. We had had classes all afternoon and I didn't feel like seeing one of the guys. I'd been with my chick all morning. I could have turned on, but I'd had it with that stuff for a while. I just stood there, and then I had this strange feeling . . . it's hard to describe, like there's nobody there. I don't mean feeling lonely or without company . . . but just not being there . . . very eerie . . ."

This young patient was describing not the massive sensation of estrangement, often found in schizophrenics, nor a total and continuous sensation of depersonalization, but a brief and partial loss of identity.

The patient was considered a better than average student by his teachers, he had a number of friends and enjoyed sexual intercourse with girls. His internal ego conflicts were manifest only when one examined the kind of friends he habitually chose: they all represented mirror images of a certain kind. All his friends were borderline personalities, not functioning in school or at home, taking drugs habitually and living continuously on the edge of trouble with the law. While he looked down on them with one part of his ego, he identified with them via the other part. This is precisely what occurs in depersonalization, where we can speak of a conflict within the ego, the part as Jacobson put it "that has accepted and the part that attempts to undo identification with a degraded object."[13]

The patient would "turn on" with these friends, while at the same time denying the experience, rationalizing that he was only "going along for the ride." When authority figures would remind him of the dangers of using drugs regularly, the patient would reassure them and himself by saying that "all my friends are doing it."

Using drugs for this patient—and other young adults I have seen— was one way to compensate for feelings of depersonalization, brief fugue states of estrangements, which, as Federn made clear, is not the same as "object-loss."[14] The difference between estrangement and object-loss can better be understood through comprehension of the "ego-boundary" concept.

Federn suggests that "the term ego-boundary shall not designate more than the existence of a perception of the extension of our ego feeling." He emphasizes that these boundaries are always changing, are not, as some writers assumed, rigid or permanent. In taking drugs, the patient's ego-boundary is less cathected with libido, so that we should expect a state of diminished affectivity. He can cope with the partial state of depersonalization, the loss of identity, via the oceanic sensation of Nirvana or omnipotence which the drugs can produce. There is enough ego-libido to perceive objects and reality so that, seen from the outside, the patient can relate to others, talk, walk, laugh.

While in younger patients, in early or middle adolescence, transference-authority or suggestion may occasionally be useful in preventing the formation of a dangerous habit—particularly when the basis is
more social than intrapsychic—in postadolescence the symptoms will
have to be completely bypassed, while all exploratory work should be
directed toward the details of the unfolding of the pathologic narcissism, i.e., a substitute for object strivings.

The young adult patient will want to use his therapist as a parent
antagonist and by producing authority reactions, repeat acting out of
his early omnipotent drives. If we can, instead, help our young adult
to become conscious of the fact that he is seeking to establish a solid
feeling of self, he will be interested in the causes of his symptom,
rather than the publicized effects.

While parents and law-enforcement figures will be mainly concerned
with the effect of this symptom, we need to direct our research toward
the diverse causes that lead young people to hallucogenic experiences,
of which states of depersonalization are one of many.

At the same time, we want to remain aware of the fact that postadolescents attempt to cope with identity diffusion in other ways, besides the brief states of depersonalization. Glover, who views identity
as a compound of ego feelings, suggests in the previously quoted
paper[12] that when the individual cannot achieve this feeling, he will
develop "reactions of symptomatic disturbances among which hysterical,
depressive and schizophrenic experiences are dominant."

While such reactions will be found among many of our adult patients who have not been able to successfully cope with the identity
conflicts, we would have some difficulty making such a definite diagnosis among our post adolescent population. Undoubtedly, the problem of differential diagnosis which we know from our adolescent
patients still continues into postadolescence and will be discussed in
the clinical part of the book.

With young adult patients we can probably be more certain of
symptoms stemming from the psychosexual conflicts involved in the
identity conflict. It is not necessary to restate the nature of the psychosexual struggle in preadolescence and at the height of puberty, since
this has been well covered in the literature, most clearly by Anna
Freud in her two chapters on puberty in *Ego and the Mechanisms of
Defence*.[16]

PSYCHOSEXUAL ASPECTS OF THE IDENTITY STRUGGLE

The nature of this aspect of the identity struggle can be gleaned by
observing its manifest content, in particular the manner in which

many young adults talk about it. The frequency and the intensity with which young adults refer to homosexuality is well known both among young men and women, but probably most contemptuously in regard to acting out male homosexuality. One might be tempted at first to explain this with the predominant cultural attitude, but then one is reminded that a few years later and throughout adult life there is both less hostility and less interest in this particular sexual manifestation. The cultural attitudes undoubtedly contribute to the young adult's hostile expressions toward homosexual behavior, but the causes would have to be sought in their own ambivalent psychosexual feelings, which are aspects of the identity struggle.

While some of the vehemence undoubtedly represents a continuation of the adolescent denial or reaction-formation defense mechanisms, there is now an urgency about the entire psychosexual identity struggle which was not as evident during adolescence. We might attribute this anxiety to the realistic awareness that the young adult has reached the point of no return in his experimentation and sexual role-playing.

Many young adults who have not yet been able to arrive at a relatively conflict-free object choice have yielded to their superego pressures and become involved in heterosexual relations, while they found the most exciting gratification in masturbation or a number of pregenital activities. Several young adult patients have reported with great distress and guilt that fantasies and masturbation, voyeuristic or exhibitionistic experiences have been more gratifying than making love to their new wife or husband.

That the psychosexual aspect of the identity struggle seems to be on the increase at this phase of development was also suggested by the change in the dream content of several young adult patients whom I had treated during the last two years of high school and who had returned during or after college. While they now were involved in heterosexual relationships, some considering permanent alignments, there was much more overt homosexual material in their dreams than before, during the height of adolescence. That they were able to bring this material and associate to it with less anxiety and more sophistication is a function of the better ego balance of this phase, but that the dreams appeared now much more prominently than before would suggest a heightened increase in cathexis and a more active struggle with the pregenital aspects of the identity struggle. The more powerful superego forces, which had been separated from the ego during adolescence, have returned and seem to bring heavy pressure to bear on the ego, demanding a decision as to their definite psychosexual identity.

What seems to be characteristic for the psychosexual aspects of the identity struggle in post adolescence is the recognition on the part of some young adults that the new permanent relationship has not affected the unresolved psychosexual conflicts of adolescence. Many young adults who had been vaguely aware of certain sexual conflicts during adolescence had assumed that, once they had arrived at a serious object choice and arranged their lives as free of conflict and guilt as possible, these problems would gradually abate.

While there may be a reduction of anxiety induced by environmental changes, the basic identity conflicts remain and will appear in the form of symptoms which are often erroneously taken as stemming from the new alliance or object choice. The subsequent interaction of symptoms frequently leads to a breakdown of newly formed relationships, accounting for the high degree of divorces in young marriages.

A young woman who had not fully resolved her primary homosexual identity had nevertheless developed enough of a feminine identity to have dates and enjoy foreplay with young men in her college. Using the old-fashioned taboo against premarital intercourse as a rationalization, her genital development had remained on the clitoral level so that orgasm was experienced through mutual masturbation and pregenital fantasies of which she was not conscious at the time. A very attractive and gifted young woman, she married a very attractive and gifted young man who had not resolved his own homosexual conflicts but had developed as his defense against it the Don Juan role, which he was playing successfully with many different girls.

Both young people were able to function with this psychosexual conflict of their identities throughout adolescence until they decided to get married and start their young adult life. The young woman at first resented the intrusion of the penis, demanding a continuation of the familiar foreplay substitute, which is essentially ego-libido instead of object-libido. It represents an autoerotic gratification with partial object relation. The young man, who had found himself fantasying about images of girls he had desired that day, took his young wife's frustration as evidence of rejection of him, the inadequate lover. Partially based on his guilt for his promiscuous activities and current fantasies, partially based on his unresolved homosexual conflicts, he developed a partial impotence which he attributed to his wife's lack of response, while the young woman took his interest in other woman as a sign of rejection of her, the inadequate lover.

These conflicts were not perceived on the level of psychosexual identity conflicts, but were acted out in the form of mutual irritation with each other, aggravation of basically minor intellectual and cultural differences, a series of small but painful acts of animosity and hostilities. When a number of economic difficulties occurred, demanding maximum cooperation between the two young people, the relationship rapidly collapsed under the pressure of these additional burdens.

Characteristically, both young people at first used the last conflicts, the economic setbacks, as explanations for their marriage breakdown but reconsidered under the advice of a counselor and viewed the difficulties as stemming from the interpersonal difficulties. Based on this assumption they separated and found new partners, with whom they repeated the same difficulties, the unresolved psychosexual aspects of their individual identity conflicts.

Neither of the two young people, nor their group of peers, were particularly disturbed by the failure of their marriage, because they considered living together as experiments that might well not succeed. This rationalization of their unresolved identity conflict covers up a more basic manifestation of postadolescence: the establishment of transitory ego-solutions consisting of partial repression, partial acting out of unresolved pregenital positions.

While the symptom formations will be different for each character structure, the common denominator seems to be their weakened reality testing, impaired by their narcissism. I have seen a large number of young people in this phase of development who seem to express in their thinking and action the idea that reality is yet to come, that this is a goal they will reach shortly, but have not quite reached as yet. Clinically this would be manifested in an all-pervading ambivalence which is readily admitted by the patient, while a close examination of the particular nature of his ambivalence is met with various forms of strong resistances: acting out, denial, projection, and even dangerous regression to psychotic states.

Case Illustration

Many of these psychosexual aspects of the identity struggle became clearer in a patient whose analysis was characterized by the particular mode of her ambivalence: a constant alternation between sublimation and repression, working through and acting out, healthy and pathologic narcissism. Throughout the different developmental phases this young woman *acted out her partially repressed wishes with substitutes,* using narcissism as a substitute for object strivings, instead of for their support.

When this very attractive young woman came to analysis at the age of twenty, she was still an active lesbian, without being able to accept this substitute as a solution of her conflicts. She had, in fact, attempted a marriage, as an "experiment," following the breakup of her latest homosexual affair.

When she realized that this marriage was failing, she had to face the psychosexual identity conflict: she could no longer continue to act out partially repressed wishes with substitutes, but had to analyze them in the transference.

Because of the patient's lifelong pattern of acting out, one had to expect strong resistances against interventions aimed at change of this pattern. With this awareness, the first phase of the analysis was essentially a learning process in which the total reality of the patient's life was included, with considerable activity on the therapist's part. The clinical problem consisted in walking the thin line between liberating energies, which are narcissistic libido, and providing the ego with adequate protection at the same time. The aim of the first phase was a sharper differentiation between ego and nonego, a reduced fluidity of ego boundaries, less projective mechanisms.

The active struggle with the psychosexual conflicts came into focus in the second phase, while the last phase is characterized by working through the pregenital conflicts.

What follows is a brief description of the three phases of the five-year analysis, after enough historical background to make the clinical material more meaningful for an illustration of the complexity of the psychosexual aspects of the identity struggle.

BACKGROUND MATERIAL: The youngest child of a lower-middle class Jewish tailor, the patient was certain that her mother's rivalry with her was responsible for her deep feelings of inadequacy, sadness and desperation. She described her mother as a self-pitying woman who had tried to make a doll out of her. The patient was winning baby contests and continued to be the kind of beauty that should become a model or a "Miss America." When she was not living up to the image of a sweet, submissive little girl, mother would treat her harshly, using a great deal of physical punishment. She speaks of "poor father" as a henpecked husband, a passive man who never openly took her side against mother, working hard into the night in his tailor shop and being seldom available for comfort. The brother, seven years older, who was on his way to the traditional role of the "doctor," lorded his intelligence and masculinity over her all through early childhood and latency. The only family member who actively took her side was her mother's brother, who showered her with presents, took her out on trips, and seduced her when she was five years old, beginning a relationship which continued into her ninth year: *the first substitution*.

The relationship to the big brother is characterized by a very brief period of active rejection of his arrogance, after which the hostility turns into the opposite: adoration of the omniscient and omnipotent male. This is her coping with the aggressor, via identification. With her peers she openly fights, outclimbing and outfighting boys, taking pride in being called a tomboy. Just before the end of latency she gives up the active competition with boys and instead takes to adoring older girls, with homosexual fantasies.

The second substitution occurs during the junior high school years, when she combines the adoration for brother and older girls in a close relationship with a talented, latent homosexual boy for whom she buys powder and lipstick and with whom she identifies. She could adore him as a genius—he was in reality a very bright, able student— without being threatened by his masculinity; in fact, he felt dependent on her since she represented a "girl friend," so important in early adolescence for status in the peer group. When this boy breaks away and has his first homosexual relationship at the start of high school, the patient begins her first lesbian relationship. Typically, she chooses a girl who is living with another lesbian, so that she will find herself again in the triangle situation.

The third substitution is the marriage to a latent homosexual, brilliant artist whose family was of substantial financial means. The young man adored her like the uncle, beat her like the mother, and was gifted like the brother.

When this last substitution failed, she needed to ask for help.

The first Rohrschach taken at this point substantiated the evidence of some autistic thinking and impaired reality testing; *"Serious confusion as to her sexual identification and states of depersonalization."*

The psychologist suggests that further regression to narcissistic and megalomanic wishes are impending, with the possibility of a break unless her ego defenses could be strengthened.

THE FIRST PHASE: Projection, magical thinking, and denial abounded during this phase, and vivid screen memories were expressed as actual experiences. The method of presenting material was highly intellectualized: Dreams and thoughts were presented and then explained by the patient, based on popular cliches, with emphatic arm movements, suggesting a public speaker trying to win the audience. The manifest content revolved around the relationship to her husband: he beat her in impulsive rage and begged for her forgiveness; he restrained her physically from going to a lecture but begged her to tell him what to do with his mother's business; he refused to give her enough money for the household but bought her an expensive fur coat. In her dreams she saw him in a state hospital and, as one of her first actual free associations, recalled her mother's suicidal attempt which had occurred early in her adolescence. She found herself dialing wrong numbers by confusing her husband's business number with her mother's home number.

As the mother-husband transference was worked through with the continued aim of ego strengthening, she found this marriage venture increasingly intolerable. With a very gradual interpretation of resistance and particularly the meaning of words, hostility toward men could be more openly expressed. Among many interesting associations was the statement: "How horrible that only women have to have babies." Her deep distrust of men was more openly verbalized and connected with the seduction episode by her uncle, without any awareness so far of her own role in this experience.

The need for remaining passive and without responsibility was also experienced in the transference, particularly when she demanded a ruling on the planned separation from her husband. When she discovered that she could not obtain this satisfaction in the transference, she acted it out by regressive *substitution:* she herself decided on the separation, left her husband and moved into an apartment with the young woman who had originally suggested my name to the patient. She repeated the oedipal wish and regression by saying to me: if you will not support me and tell me what to do, you do not love me, so that I have no choice but to return to the woman who sent me to you. If father does not love me the way I want him to, I have no choice but to return to mother.

Throughout the two years during which she shared the apartment with this somewhat older woman, the patient behaved toward her very much as she had toward her mother. The roommate demanded and got the room with the better view, the better bed, more privacy. She demanded and got cooperation and assistance from the patient, without reciprocating. She sat her down for long lectures and critical evaluation of her behavior to which the patient responded with intellectualization, hidden hostility, and guilt. It never occurred to her to really question the soundness of her roommate's assumption, although she was able to pout and conform like an angry child. She then would report her anger about the woman in our sessions, expecting the therapist—like father—to take her side.

Characteristically for the intelligent postadolescent, she would rely on pseudoinsights by calling her demands "oedipal complex," while the real oedipal feelings were still deeply repressed and were acted out instead of remembered.

With more reality testing and subsequent lessening of fluidity of ego boundaries, she took more responsibility in her realistic life situation as well as in therapy. She recognized the need for more lucrative employment as a realistic step toward greater independence from mother, or other supporting figures. She found employment appropriate for her chosen field of work.

In therapy she too began to work with more deliberation; the facile explanation of dreams ceased, there was much less talk about things happening to her (move from passive to active), and free association became the means of communication with the analyst.

When the seduction episode came back in recurring dreams, she began to discover that there too she had relied on passivity as a defense by clinging to the version that she had been "seduced," while now the dreams clearly revealed in vivid detail her active participation in this episode. With this recognition she could begin to re-experience some aspects of the oedipal situation, ushering in the second phase of her analysis.

THE SECOND PHASE: The resistance again took the familiar form of acting out with substitutes, except that part of the material stems now from the transference so that she could become more realistic about her activities. The oedipal wishes were verbalized in the form of attempts to seduce the analyst and when, as she put it, "nothing happens here but talk," she announced that she was going to spoil the analysis by sleeping with girls again.

Here the ambivalence over the psychosexual identity was clearly expressed when she said that what she really wanted was to be a "true lesbian," only to admit in the same session that this did not seem to be "the answer" either. She had a few brief homosexual experiences which left her as unsatisfied and puzzled as before.

Still unable to resolve the ambivalence and still seeking for circumvention and acting out with substitutes, she tried another route: she had an affair with an older man whom she had known for years. With a giggle, which suggested her partial awareness of the mechanism, she confessed that this man was not just any nice man—he was the boy friend of the homosexual boy for whom she had bought lipstick in high school.

The contrast between the two levels of operation, the acting out and the working through, was vividly experienced in the session in which she reported the affair with this particular man. While she seemed flirtatious and cynical about this affair (and about having teased some girls with lesbian implications), she cried for the first time in any of her sessions as she reported that she had had her first orgasm by intercourse. Perhaps, she thought, she was a woman after all.

As if to test her new identity in the most charged area, the oedipal conflicts, she now discovered that her place of work was only a few blocks from her father's business, so that she easily could have lunch with him occasionally. During this phase of her reality testing, she found memories about father and herself that had been hidden until now. No longer did she need to talk about father as a shadowy figure who was too busy to take her side against the difficult mother, but could recall pleasant times and good experiences with him. Working back from more recent experiences at preadolescence with trips to the zoo, boat rides and picnics with father, she eventually went back to the fourth and third year. She could recall vivid details about waking up at night when father returned from his night-shift job to eat a snack with him. These experiences stopped abruptly at the beginning of the fifth year when the seduction episode with the uncle began.

The emerging of material from the end of the oedipal period was experienced in the transference through a growing trust in the therapist, together with undisguised sexual dreams in which the therapist is used as the father-uncle-love object. The other major dream theme was the wish for father's or the therapist's baby together with the open admission of penis envy and competitiveness of the male. In reality, this is experienced with two successive love affairs with young men of her own age, and this then is followed by the factual statement that "lesbianism is not the answer."

With increasing ego controls we get such realistic changes as a more responsible position in her place of work and the beginning of serious academic studies which had been neglected until now. Equally significant for the emerging sense of identity was a more realistic appraisal of her mother, and with it a lessening of her role as a child with the roommate whom she had used as a mother substitute. She gradually demanded more equality in her living arrangements, which eventually led to the breakup of this relationship and the establishment of her own home. She noted with surprise and satisfaction that this was the first time in her life that her own name was on the mailbox, a small but significant discovery of her identity.

A Rohrschach test, taken three years after the first one, suggests that she is actively and constructively coping with the demands of her environment, had considerable freedom of self-expression and ability to examine her reactions without concomitant anxiety. "In conclusion," the report reads, "the present test protocols are impressively different from those previously obtained in one very important aspect: There is no longer any evidence of autistic thinking or of a breakdown in her capacity for reality testing. She can be constructively self-critical without giving way to a feeling of helplessness and dependency."

With this indication of a definite move toward healthy narcissism and the beginning of nonincestuous object relations, with the evidence of a reduction in her ambivalence, in brief, a more integrated ego structure, the last phase of her analysis could begin: the attempted resolution of the pregenital conflicts.

THE THIRD PHASE: The material of this phase is particularly pertinent for an understanding of the struggle for identity in postadolescence, since I had defined this concept as a process that emerges out of the earliest attempts toward autonomy and a separation from incestuous objects. The mode of this patient's ambivalence which had prevented the formation of an ego-syntonic identity became clear through the dreams and associations of this phase of her analysis.

Since she was now functioning without the many disturbing conflicts in her current life—in her home, her job, her relations to mother and father, as well as brother, all of whom she could see more realistically—it was possible to concentrate on the one major difficulty: the boy friend, which gave us the opportunity to get to the pregenital material. That she could stay with this material for nearly six months, with carry-over from session to session, indicated the state of the ego.

The boy friend was a young man, a few years older than the patient, who had obtained a separation from his wife a few months earlier. From the start, the patient was attracted and disturbed by him, because he reminded her of the seductive uncle of her fifth year.

This association, which suggested still another substitution, led us to some origins of her difficulties, because it revealed the unconscious meaning of the seduction episode.

In a dream of this period she saw her diaphragm with two holes, to which her association was "now orgasm was impossible." One was struck by this association for many reasons, but most important for the fact that she had experienced orgasm in other ways than intercourse, in her lesbian relationships and by masturbation by men. Probably the first of these men was the uncle who came to mind in the chain of associations following this dream.

The historical period in which this material was re-experienced was suggested by the associations to the "two holes" in the diaphragm dream. Only the vagina came to mind to explain one "hole," and there was no explanation for the other "hole." Jones suggests that "the anus is evidently identified with the vagina to begin with, and the differentiation of the two is an extremely obscure process, more so perhaps than any other in female development. I surmise, however, that it takes place in part at an earlier age than is generally supposed."[17]

The next associations were memories of playing "having a baby on the toilet" with a girl friend. Both the undifferentiated concept of body opening and the version of the anal baby put this material in the preoedipal period.

She had apparently avoided facing her femininity at this period, using passivity as a defense against castration anxiety and penis envy. The original masturbation had been vaginal, the clitoris was not touched, nor did she ever gratify her uncle's demand to touch his penis. As some of this material is interpreted, we get such castration material as a torn lining in her coat, dreams about ripped garments, loss of front teeth, in rapid succession.

She hated the uncle but permitted him to play with her sexually, using the passive defense to avoid the onslaught of guilt. In the present she calls her boy friend an irresponsible person who "uses" her, but there is also the conscious fantasy that she is being "protected."

Although the oedipal material is there—seductive fantasies about the therapist, dreams of father's baby, hostility against therapist's wife and family—the more basic roots of the psychosexual conflict become clear only after a short, significant dream which was thoroughly analyzed.

The session starts with the announcement: "I don't know why I continue to see Hal" (the boy friend) and is followed by the dream:

"As I am getting up from the couch, you are handing me a red, velvet cape. This is very exciting, almost like orgasm. I am angry that I had this dream."

The day residue is from seeing an exhibit of this cape, worn by the singer Ezio Pinza at Bergdorf Goodman on Fifth Avenue. The excitement stems from the idea of the therapist touching her shoulders, because this is what her father had done just last week when he had measured her for a dress he was making for her. Asked for a closer connection between a dress and the dream cape, she had a vivid recollection about a cape and the wife of the seductive uncle.

Shortly after the sexual games with the uncle had ended at around nine years of age, the patient had had a raincape which she had worn one day while visiting this uncle and his wife at their house. She had left the apartment with the aunt. As she entered the elevator after her aunt, the automatic door closed and caught a corner of the cape. At the same time the elevator descended. The cape tightened around her neck since it was fastened with a hook and eye. She had the feeling of being strangled. The aunt tore the cape off her neck.

"She nearly saved my life" says the patient, as she continues to associate to the dream and suddenly feels very close to this aunt, who, the patient now feels, was a very kind woman, "much nicer than mother." It seems to the patient now, fifteen years later, that this aunt must always have been a very disturbed woman or she could not have stayed with this uncle all these years. There are more memories about daily visits to the aunt when she was three and four years old, up to the time when the sexual episode began. From then on she saw little of the aunt, considering her an "intruder" since the uncle had repeated the illusion that the patient was more desirable and beautiful than his wife.

By denying her own aggression she was able to project it on the aunt-mother and thus maintain the early narcissism, which was supported by the uncle.

In this way the pregenital fixations were maintained, while the guilt and the incest taboo were avoided, seriously interfering with her entire psychosexual development and leading to the identity crisis in post-adolescence. It is of interest to note that the guilt became manifest at the cape episode when she felt strangled, while in reality she had both the strength and the coordination to rip off the cape by herself. She needed to feel that the aunt was rescuing her. Apparently this episode had been traumatic and was repressed until this session in which it reappeared as one of the important associations to the dream, fifteen years later.

Since the aunt had in reality been helpful—both before and after the episode—it would have been difficult for the patient to think of her as an "intruder." She had to repress the episode to maintain the patho-logic narcissistic balance and, with it, strengthened the omnipotent fantasies: I am safe and all-powerful. The omnipotent mother image of pregenital times is re-experienced and the oedipal wishes are acted out with aunt's husband, the first substitute. The search for older protecting women then continued in high school and in the lesbian relationships.

The whole situation is now re-experienced through the dream and the associations in the transference: the boy friend representing the uncle, the therapist her father. It is father who touches her shoulders when he measures her for a suit; it is the therapist who hands her the exhibitionistic (male actor's) cape.

The dream and the associations to it begin to make it possible for the patient to re-experience the situation in the transference. In objectifying it in the present, she is beginning to move beyond the pre-genital mother fixation, to reduce acting out of omnipotent fantasies by substitution, and to give up the boy friend, who in time is replaced with men who no longer represent primary figures, to the point where she could marry and have a child.

The psychosexual aspects of her identity struggle seemed to have been worked through, since, on follow up she did not return to the symptom of Lesbianism.

The case was described in some detail because it illustrated both major aspects of the identity diffusion in postadolescence: states of depersonalization and psychosexual conflicts. Both aspects suggest that the uneven pace of ego integration and drive organization give the struggle for identity a particular aspect during postadolescence, as stated at the beginning of the chapter.

3. The End of Role-playing and Time Continuity

UNTIL POSTADOLESCENCE, the purpose of role-playing, as all playing, had been basically an attempt to assimilate anxiety, to gradually master reality, to prepare for more functional sublimation. The analytic literature on the function of play traces the gradual change in roles through the different libidinal phases as a substitute for several incompletely developed functions of the ego, including the body-ego. To take the phase that directly precedes postadolescence, we know how the adolescent substitutes for the incomplete integration of the ego, the heterosexual conflicts, the work-play struggle, by typically seizing a role or a function that he can comfortably handle and which serves to get him by with both peers and the adult demands. He behaves the way many people do in situations where they are ill at ease: They cover up the anxiety with some—perhaps helpful—activity, to achieve a temporary balance. The adolescent plays a number of roles: "the strong-silent type," the "cool character," "the bored or the naive type"—transitory manifestations of his attempts to cope with anxiety.

In postadolescence this is more and more difficult, because where the identity conflicts and the self-image dilemma intersect, role-playing becomes nearly impossible. Both the struggle for a persistent experience of sameness and the ego-ideal versus superego conflicts, together with the alignments with the reference group and the socioeconomic pressures, demand that the young adult take a permanent role which is to be his and which can no longer be changed without new and often painful anxiety in adult life.

Until this point in the life cycle, it was to some degree possible for the identity struggle and the self-image dilemma to coexist. They both would intrude on the ego balance during various times in adolescence, but could be kept separated, i.e., the adolescent could get comfort from having solved one or the other battle for the time being. Success in some areas of study or work, gratification from peers within his reference group, strong acceptance by a member of the opposite sex—any satisfactions in one of the important areas, however temporary, will usually be enough to keep the identity struggle and the self-image dilemma from coming into dangerously close contact. The adolescent

26

can still play the role of the successful student, the popular candidate, the attractive femme fatale—even though he or she may sense that this is a role which "will do" for the time being, might change pretty quickly, might mean little in the future "when I go out into the world."

The need to keep the identity diffusion and the self-image separate is expressed in adolescence in many characteristic ways of behaving. The most common is the need to keep certain friends from knowing other friends. This is understandable if we recognize that the adolescent often plays different roles in different friendship groups, roles which reflect either the identity conflict or the self-image dilemma. If you would ask the adolescent why it is so important that his friends from the tennis court do not get to know his old pals back home whom he sees once a week, he will tell you that he is "different" with the athletes than with the "cornballs" from old Hometown. He may put it in sociologic terms: he may call one group "highbrow" and another "lowbrow" and say he would feel embarrassed to belong to both. Actually this does not explain very much since youngsters from either group will form their own judgment about each other, independent of the feelings of the young man who wants to keep them apart. Not only does he want to keep them from knowing each other, he may dress, act, sound differently, or be addressed by different nicknames in different groups. He plays different roles in adolescence and dreads the time when this will no longer be possible.

Postadolescence is ushered in by a somewhat frantic return to the pleasure principle, by a last-minute attempt to avoid the firmer cathexis of ego boundaries, a sometimes bizarre, sometimes sad attempt to hold off the coming of the inevitable recognition of reality limitations. There is in the postadolescent phase some element of mourning, aspects of grief and depression. This is expressed in many typical attempts to create something "new and different," to look and sound "young," no matter how absurd even to the rational aspect of the young man or woman their behavior may appear. Anything but "reality," which is taken to mean a humdrum, conventional, "square" existence, with neither excitement nor individuality. If the identity struggle and the self-image dilemma are too turbulent, the young adult often experiences panic states at the prospect of going through the long life ahead "just like anybody else." In these cases the kind of roles that he is playing often points to diagnostic clues. Some young adults actually verbalize the anxiety when they say: "I'll try anything, except the boring nine to five existence you see all around you."

This does not necessarily point to unresolved oedipal problems—although in the last analysis this is probably valid—but unless we can understand the postadolescent variations of the basic conflicts, we cannot be of much help to young people.

What the young adult fears is not altogether unrealistic or neurotic. What had kept him buoyant had been the special privileges accorded to youth in our culture, particularly in adolescence. He had been told a hundred times to hitch his wagon to a star, to dream big dreams, to venture out, to try everything and experiment all over the map. Nobody held him to it when his ideas turned out to be faulty because of lack of depth, when his fantastic experiments did not succeed, when he acknowledged that he had been wrong. No matter what role he played, he was assured of survival: there would still be food, a place to sleep, the basic creature comforts. Is the young adult unrealistic if he acknowledges that all this assurance of security will shortly terminate; that the basic necessities will not be provided any more by family, school or government; that he—and he alone—will have to rely on his own providence and assure his survival? If, with this realistic view by the functioning ego, he is torn by deep doubts about his identity ("I don't even know what I'm all about"), by the self-image conflicts ("Do I do what is really right for me or do I do what I should do?")—if these conflicts overlap and flood the intact parts of the ego, we can understand that the recognition of the end of role-playing represents still another specific characteristic of postadolescence.

Where the adolescent laughed problems off, the postadolescent feels weighed down by them. For a time, daring is replaced by timidity, spontaneity by ponderousness, elation by depression. When the postadolescent asks for therapy, we will need to distinguish between genuine character disorders and this postadolescent syndrome, which, like mourning, may not necessarily require therapeutic intervention. The administration of projective tests may help here with differential diagnosis.

That role-playing is coming to an end was expressed by a senior in college when she said: "I'm not worried about the marks, what scares me is the finalty of these tests. Everything you put down now is for real."

The recognition of the postadolescent state is experienced as a narcissistic injury, a demand by the outside world, a threat to the unconscious omnipotent fantasies, a final testing of the long-cherished illusions about the "high potential." Where the ego boundaries—particularly between ego and superego[18]—were not firm in the first place, we may expect regression and symptom-formation, reactivated by the only partially resolved identity conflict and self-image dilemma.

COGNITION OF TIME CONTINUITY

The student who said that she was concerned about the "finality" of the tests also illustrated the anxiety about the cognition of time continuity, which may be called still another characteristic of postadolescence. It is implied in "the end" of role-playing, suggesting limitations, beginning and end, continuity of time. The concept of time, as a measurable aspect of duration, is of course subject to the same laws of reality perception as other abstract concepts. Aspects of the pleasure principle will interfere with the full recognition of time lived—or time left for pleasure—because of the direct connection with pathologic narcissism. Children get angry at the clock, the inevitable movement of the second hand, which spells out limitation of pleasure at the moment. Adolescents often increase their omnipotent fantasies by not wearing a watch. They may tell you that they don't need to be reminded of time all day long. "It makes me feel too tied down." They feel "timeless," symbolic for uncathected ego boundaries, similar to the young adult on LSD who will feel "weightless." He was describing the oceanic feeling of floating in space, unhampered by any limitations, by inner boundaries, matter or time.

While such manifestations are extreme, some of these aspects seem to be experienced by many young people during postadolescence, because this is the period of growth when the concept of time intrudes more forcefully on the ego than before.

As the reality principle gradually crowds out the pleasure principle in early childhood, the gradual recognition of time—future as an extension of the present—characterizes adolescence and reaches its sometimes critical climax in postadolescence. The typical defense mechanisms, avoiding, postponing, forgetting, to mention some of the most characteristic ones, are accepted as part of the adolescent struggle. In postadolescence we notice a significant change, because reality is no longer experienced via authority figures—which could be defied until now—but by the natural consequences of one's actions. The effects of the young adult's actions—as compared to the actions of the adolescent—are long range. Where the young man in high school can safely oversleep a class or two, the graduate student, who may hold a teaching fellowship, can no longer afford to keep his first-year students waiting. If he depends on scholarships for his graduate study—as many young people do—the difference between a B or an A as an average mark may mean the difference between a few thousand dollars in income the following year. While a young man in college can safely sign his name to a piece of paper—knowing that some adult may ultimately be held accountable—the young adult who signs his name to his first apartment lease knows that he, and he alone, will be held accountable. A few young adults have expressed considerable anxiety about this kind of long-range planning: four years of graduate study or a two-year apartment lease. The idea of committing yourself for more than a few months seems frightening to many postadolescents.

There seems to be a cut-off point at the end of the junior year or the start of the senior year in college, when most young adults feel that they have come to the end of the road of adolescence and a semiprotected existence. Still struggling with the identity concept, torn by the self-image dilemma, at the end of role-playing, they now experience the full impact of the time continuity, as representatives of business and industry appear on the campus to recruit employees, offering contracts and expecting performance. Professional scholarships for graduate study are available, requiring long-range commitments, definite choices of professions, careers, schools, places to live, financing, realistic planning. Although the adolescent has known about these future commitments for a long time, although high school and college have intellectually prepared him for this time, the postadolescent often experiences the reality of the time continuity only now as he asks himself—or is asked: What are you going to do with your life?

Fantasies about time, magical thinking in connection with the time concept (as earlier with numbers) are common during adolescence, but it seems that only during the postadolescence phase young people make firm contact with the time limitation, as one as yet uncathected ego boundary. Often the concept is experienced not so much in terms of the future—time ahead—but in terms of the past—time gone. This experience was made very vivid for me through the associations of a patient, a young man in his early twenties, who went through a near panic experience when the anxiety about the time concept had been innocently triggered by a colleague. This young man had been a borderline patient with mild paranoid fantasies who had gone through a long analysis and was well on his way to full recovery. While talking with a fellow physicist about time, first in theoretic, then practical terms during a lunch break in the laboratory in which both were employed, the colleague happened to ask the patient how old he was, and expressed surprise about the fact that the patient was "already twenty-three years old."

The patient's inner reaction to this common inquiry is best shown in his own words.

"I didn't say anything much to Tom about it and changed the subject until we went back to work, but once I was at my desk I could hardly sit still, I was so upset and although I told myself that I was acting stupid, I couldn't help myself . . . all the old fears of dying, of the idea of getting old—ridiculous as it sounds—came back full force and hit me smack in the center of the head . . . I mean, the whole thing was so crazy, I know how old I am, I have my degree, my own apartment, my car, I'm an adult . . . I pay my rent, my insurance and all . . . but it didn't help . . . knowing what's real . . . that people get surprised when they learn my age . . . because I look so young, I look like a kid, can't get a drink in some bars without my draft card . . . that always sets me off, except this time it was worse . . . almost a third of my life gone . . . only two-thirds more to go . . . I mean, that's true by insurance statistics . . . that there is nothing you can do about it . . . about time passing, about getting older and eventually dying . . . it stayed with me all that day and most of the night . . . I woke up every few hours, in cold sweat . . . I'm still shaky about it . . . you want to yell: stop . . . yell at the clock . . . the way the second hand goes round and round . . . you want to go back to the time when things were taken care of for you . . . but you realize that it just goes on . . . you're in it . . . for real . . . it just goes on and on . . . time just continues . . ."

For this patient the fuller recognition of time continuity included the re-experiencing of such early fears as desertion anxiety, the panic of being abandoned—fears against which he had protected himself with magical thinking and other omnipotent fantasies. While his reaction is determined by his particular pathology, the process of fully integrating the reality of the time continuity is a characteristic struggle for most young people in postadolescence, because it is only now that the concept is forcefully brought home. One of the major factors which contribute to the sharper recognition of time is the economic reality of the young adult's life. We shall discuss them in more detail in the subsequent section of the book, where some of the sociologic aspects will be covered.

The fuller recognition of the time continuity also complicates the self-image dilemma and may have some bearing on some of the particular identity conflicts that we discussed earlier.

We can readily understand this connection if we remember how much age has been associated with achievement all through early childhood, latency, and adolescence. While the obsession with time as a measure of achievement is a learned response—imposed by the world of parents and teachers—it is readily taken into the superego or the ego-ideal and will play a part in the self-image dilemma in postadolescence. The ability to read is valued more highly in a four- than in a five-year-old child; skipping a grade is usually considered a sign of maturity by parents and by the child, whether this is indicated by his ego integration or not. To arrive at the third grade at seven instead of eight years of age means a narcissistic satisfaction for the parent and usually for the child; to enter high school or college at an earlier age than the majority of students becames part of the superego, when parents or teachers emphasize the time factor as significant in the achievement. Gradually time comes to represent value, marking definite superego demands and standards: at eighteen you graduate from high school, at twenty-two from college with a bachelor's degree, at twenty-five you should be married—a chain of incorporated demands as definite and impersonal as the timetable of an airline.

Until postadolescence this timetable was as much taken for granted as a roof over the young adult's head, as his daily meals or spending allowance. Only now, as the time continuity is fully recognized as a measure of duration determinable by the ego, does the young adult begin to question the pace of his studies, his work, his own life. It is, as one young adult put it, like your first solo flight, when nobody tells you how fast to fly and nobody but you, yourself, is at the controls.

The young adult who has fully recognized the extension of time, the time continuity into the future, also discovers that he determines the way he uses the time ahead.

What is better for him (his self-image, the way he sees himself, the way he would like to be seen): to stop his studies and settle down at the lucrative job offered, or to put in four more years of study for the goal that represents his ego-ideal? Should he listen to the practical advice of his father or a certain counselor—follow the super-ego demands—or would he be happier if he did what would be "right" for him, regardless of what anybody says—following his ego-ideal? The self-image dilemma and the time-continuity recognition clearly intersect at this juncture. And if we re-read the previous sentence, with the accent on "right for *him*," we realize how this matter of time continuity also has bearing on the identity conflicts.

In particular, it directly affects both the brief states of depersonalization and the psychosexual conflicts, which we discussed in the previous chapter. Perhaps we can visualize this complication better if we think of the many demands made on the ego of the young adult in terms of energy distribution, comparable to a man aiming to do justice to more tasks or individuals than he can afford to do. As the postadolescent gradually recognizes the reality of time continuity, he is moving from pathologic to healthy narcissism; he is cathecting his ego boundaries more solidly. This task requires a total libidinal investment in order to cope with the often depressing awareness of limitations, as illustrated with the young physicist who had been asked about his age. This leaves little libidinal energy for coping with the "persisting experience of sameness"—the limited definition of identity we had used for operational purposes. In other words, the young adult may fully recognize that life goes on, but not necessarily that he, himself, continues as part of it. This then opens the regressive path to depersonalization states in which parts of the self—ego or body parts—are decathected and experienced as "not belonging to me." It is like shedding luggage in an overloaded ship. Something has to give, and it is frequently the identity struggle.

It may work the other way around as well: The postadolescent may use his energy to cope with the identity struggle and the self-image dilemma and postpone the full recognition of time continuity or the end of role-playing to a later date in his life. He may say, "I don't think that far ahead."

The psychosexual aspects of the identity struggle are also linked to the recognition of time continuity in postadolescence—in particular, the establishment of transitory ego-solutions, consisting of partial repression, partial acting out of unresolved pregenital positions.

We had suggested that many young people in this phase of development seem to express in their thinking and their actions the idea that reality is yet to come, that this is a goal they shall reach before long, but have not reached as yet.

As the time continuity is more fully recognized, it becomes more difficult to withdraw to this defense, with the result that pregenital acting out increases in a somewhat desperate attempt to stay the inevitable necessity of fully squaring up to reality. What is commonly referred to as "settling down" means the full recognition of the end of role-playing, the acceptance of the time continuity and the effect of these limitations on the self-image dilemma and the identity struggle of adolescence. Both depersonalization and psychosexual conflicts are aggravated by the intersection of these developments, but perhaps the most conspicuous aspect of the latter is seen in the search for a permanent love object, the topic of the following chapter.

4. The Search for the Partner

WHILE THE PREVIOUS characteristics of postadolescence all represented aspects of intrapsychic conflicts, the fifth characteristic adds a new dimension: the choice of a love object, and one which differs from all other object choices in the sense that it is conceived as leading to a permanent and hopefully lifelong affiliation. In postadolescence the object choice becomes the search for the partner. It is the most demanding test of ego-integration, the intactness of ego boundaries, the degree to which healthy narcissism functions as countercathexis for omnipotent strivings, instead of as their substitute, as Federn suggested.

This search for the partner comes at a time when many young adults are still struggling with the identity crisis, beset by occasional states of depersonalization; it occurs in the midst of the attempt to resolve the self-image dilemma, when many postadolescents move from ego-ideal to superego demands; it interferes with the recognition of the end of role-playing and the time continuity. For some young adults the search for the partner complicates the psychosexual conflicts, which, as we have suggested, are not always resolved by this time.

The search for the partner then comes at a time when the young adult is still very much preoccupied with intrapsychic struggles, which theoretically all would have to have been resolved before an ego-syntonic object choice could be expected. That so many couples find it too difficult to resolve their difficulties is understandable if one only thinks of the fact that this far-reaching, highly complex search for the life partner is expected by our culture of two young people who very often have not been able to get their own individual house in order.

When we discuss some of the social aspects of postadolescence, we shall have more to say about the causes of the subtle pressures on the young adult who expects himself to find a partner now. If we consider this characteristic as the culmination of the previous inner demands on the young adult, we can truly speak of postadolescence as the period of the greatest pressure in terms of completion of partially finished integration tasks. We cannot expect most young adults to have fulfilled all the requirements for this final test of maturity. Indeed we would be more realistic if we assumed that many of the young adult partnerships cannot be based on sufficiently integrated ego structures.

Where the identity crisis is still mainly unresolved, the young adult may not be able to search for a partner, but search for a love object with which to merge, with which to reconstitute the lost object of the "primary identification." Frequently these young people look for and find mirror images, that is, postadolescents of the opposite sex who, likewise, attempt to recapture the fantasy of the nurturing breast they never had. These merging relationships of course will have to lead to depressing frustration and after a short while turn out to be more pain than pleasure, often to be given up and replaced by another phantom relationship, based on the same need for merging.

Young adults who are in the midst of the self-image dilemma frequently abandon the difficult resolution of this struggle and hope to form instead a satisfying relationship with the opposite sex, which turns out to be a substitute for the unresolved self-image dilemma. The partner is to represent the ego-ideal or the superego, depending on the nature of his internal struggle. The relationship is based on the partner's ability to function as ego-ideal or superego substitute, a role that can be played for a certain time and under limited circumstances. Typically, the partner will have to prove a disappointment, since he or she cannot take the place of the unresolved self-image dilemma any more than he can make up for a physiologic or academic lack.

Where the end of role-playing or recognition of the time continuity has not been fully integrated, the search for the partner too will be used as a substitute for incomplete inner resolutions and will have to lead to painful separations once the playing-house role, for example, is ended by the request for financial responsibility. The arrival of a baby, for example, often proves too real a demand for the insufficiently integrated ego, signaling the beginning of the end of the relationship.

Wherever the search for the partner is not ego-syntonic, it cannot lead to realistic gratification but has to usher in various degrees of regression and substitute solutions.

Again, the culture and the particular historic phase of development—with emphasis on passive and pleasure principle gratifications—offers a face-saving device to the young adult. This device is the ceremonial or the ritual accompanying the legalizing of the substitute solutions. Whenever the young adult finds himself unable to cope with the multiple inner demands that have to be met prior to the search for the partner, he can choose the high-status, culturally sanctioned, family-and-church-endorsed institution of marriage.

ESCAPE INTO MARRIAGE

The escape into marriage often is in reality a substitute solution in the complex search for the partner. It serves as a temporary shortcut for many of the unresolved postadolescent struggles. Although many young adults are at moments aware of the temporary nature of the affiliation, they cannot resist the temptation to experiment, particularly since the outside world rewards them with gifts and reassures them, stilling for a time the many realistic inner doubts.

We can better understand how the escape into marriage can be used as an attempt to avoid the postadolescence struggles if we take each of the characteristics and observe in some detail how the formalizing of a sexual relationship may serve the purpose of circumventing the inner conflicts.

1. *The self-image crisis*

The self-image crisis, which we had defined as a conflict between ego-ideals and superego, can be avoided by the escape-into-marriage gambit. The most common illustration is the young man who feels that he should marry the girl he has been living with or the girl who is expecting him to marry her. By formalizing his relationship he seems to have ended the postadolescent struggle of what is right for him and what his models expect of him. By acting out the superego demands he will gain temporary peace. He will have bought this respite by avoiding the self-image dilemma, but at the same time he has increased the ambivalent mode of his behavior. Instead of vascillating between ego-ideals and superego, as we had suggested, this young man will alternately love and hate his wife or their child.

For other young adults this "escape into marriage" may create serious complications in the ego balance later in life, when they discover that the ego-ideal demands—which seemed to have been stilled— have remained intact and make a tumultuous comeback, just when it seems as though the reliance on the superego had been a solution of the self-image dilemma.

While the manifest reasons for the dissolution of the marriage often appear to be in the interaction between two partners, it would seem after more incisive analytic investigation that the deeper causes can be found in the unresolved self-image dilemma of one or both partners. The reliance on ego-ideals or the superego, to the extent that one had been neglected, usually leads to deep frustration and often resentment via projection on the partner, as though it was he or she who had precipitated the substitute: escape into marriage. The man who finds himself unable to pursue his artistic needs—following his ego-ideal demands—will blame his wife for his lack of time, of energy, of concentration. The man who has followed these ego-ideal demands to the exclusion of the superego, will try to turn away from the superego demands by avoiding contact with all those aspects in his daily life that tend to evoke the unfulfilled responsibilities toward his wife or family. Withdrawal or defiantly bizarre behavior may become his defense against the pain of the unresolved self-image dilemma.

Still another manner in which the escape into marriage can be used as an avoidance of the painful self-image dilemma can be observed in the way in which the partner is used. Freud suggested that "that which he projects ahead of him as his ideal is merely his substitute for the lost narcissism of his own childhood—the time when he was his own ideal." And he continues in this same paper[5] that "the narcissism that now seems to be displaced on this new ego-ideal deems itself the possessor of all perfections."

When this is projected on the love object, the partner becomes the incarnation of the ego-ideal, a restitution of the original narcissistic position, in which a parent had been cast in the role which now the new partner has to play. With this projection of the early narcissistic ego-ideal on the partner, or by perhaps merging with him, the young adult, far from having resolved her self-image dilemma, will be able to function for a time in this illusionary state. This should not be confused with the adoring wife or husband, who seem unable to be critical of their chosen partner. The projection of the ego-ideal on the partner is a much more subtle development, not nearly as open to observation as the uncritical husband. The process is in the main not observable because it has not taken place on the level of consciousness. With young people who have not been analyzed, this development may reach on some rare occasions preconscious awareness, perhaps after a stormy scene or other unsettling moments. What takes place in the interaction between two young people in this state of ego-ideal projection is this: when the husband does not live up to the image of the projected ego-ideal, the young wife becomes depressed, because she experiences his lack of success as her failure in order to keep the ego-ideal projection intact. He must remain on his pedestal for the projection to work or else the young wife would have to face her self-image dilemma, which she could not bear to consider in the first place. She will find explanation for her husband's failure: her lack of understanding, her demands on him, her bad advice.

It is different when the partner has been used for a superego projection. In this case the young wife will get very angry at the husband who had to play the role of the projected inner censor, the harsh authority whom she had followed, only to be let down. She clings to her ego-ideal—which often will be a pseudoideal—giving the whole responsibility for lack of success or any difficulties to the husband, who had been the carrier of her projected superego. Again, for her to consider her own responsibility—to face up to her own displaced super-ego—would mean having to arrive at a compromise between ego-ideal and superego, or a resolution of the self-image dilemma, the very thing she had hoped to avoid by the escape into marriage.

To the extent to which the ego-ideal can be considered as "the common ideal of a family, class or nation," as Freud suggested in the same paper, the escape into marriage may serve the same function as in the other situations mentioned above: avoidance of the self-image dilemma. This was made startlingly clear to me by a patient who had entered into a marriage to avoid both the self-image dilemma and the identity crisis. In order to continue the merging relationship with her mother, this young woman repeated her childhood status in her relationship with her boy friend, whom she married because this was the ideal state of existence, according to the mother, grandmother and the tightly knit community in which she had grown up.

Although she had long been aware that she "should" not be in this hostile dependency relationship, that she should not be married at all, at this point of her life, but finish her ambitious career, she continued in this role until her mother died. Only four weeks after her mother's funeral, she announced in her therapeutic session that she did not think divorce was that terrible a step to take as she had always been led to believe. It took her mother's death to free her to the point where she could face the self-image dilemma and work toward an ego-syntonic solution.

Until this point, the status of being a married woman, to be called "Mrs.," seemed to be a resolution of the self-image quandary. Where the dilemma had been keenly experienced before the marriage in everyday decision-making, in arriving at simple choices, she could now use the status of being married to avoid decisions or choices, by referring them to her husband. These had been the gratifications which made it possible for her to tolerate the unsatisfactory relationship. Once her mother was no longer there as a living model, the patient could face the reality of this marriage and work toward a more fulfilling situation. She was aware that she gave up some of the substitute gratification of being somebody's wife, but as she herself put it, "It wasn't worth the trouble. I'll be making lots of mistakes, but at least they'll be my own."

2. *Aspects of the identity struggle*

When we had discussed this characteristic of postadolescence, we had referred to the concept of "identity" as "a struggle toward a persistent experience of sameness, a process of the ego that emerges out of the earliest attempts toward autonomy, toward separation from the original symbiotic state and incestuous objects." We suggested that the young adult may have a self-representation, an acceptable mode of coping with drive cathexes and a partial resolution of bisexual conflicts, although we had emphasized the problem of object choices had to be solved. When the uneven drive organization and the ego-integration struggle become too much, we had suggested the formation of a number of symptoms of which brief states of depersonalization seem to be characteristic.

Where the adolescent may try to counteract such disturbing sensations by close attachment to friends, who represent mirror images, the postadolescent can create the illusion of a persistent quality of sameness by merging with a love object, which society assures him will always be available, as long as he takes the responsibility of fidelity.

The substitute aspect of this relationship becomes clear when the tenuous balance between two insufficiently developed ego structures is upset and the union threatens to collapse. Each of the partners finds himself suddenly without an identity, experiencing sometimes serious states of depersonalization, panic-like anxiety states or passive regressions.

A patient who found herself in this state of disorganization made the dynamics of this situation clear when she said, "Without Bill in the house there is nobody there. When I passed the mirror in the bedroom without thinking, I was suddenly scared because it seemed for a moment that there was somebody in the room. I realized of course that this was me, but it didn't mean anything, because I don't exist without Bill holding me."

The phrase "holding me" or "being held" occurs over and over again in these relationships which serve as substitutes for insufficiently developed identity states, pointing to the pregenital phase of the early ego and the need to exist in a near symbiotic state with the object.

In this patient one could also observe insufficiently developed aspects of the psychosexual aspects of the identity crisis, which we had mentioned and illustrated in one case in an earlier chapter. For this young woman being married to Bill meant for a time that the sexual identity struggle had been solved, since she now was "a married woman." Actually, she had not reached genital primacy, but tolerated penetration as a somewhat unpleasant, necessary byproduct of an otherwise all-sheltering security operation, as symbolized in the statement: "I don't exist without Bill holding me." When the marriage broke up, she returned to masturbation with vaguely disguised homosexual fantasies, indicating to what degree the "escape into marriage" had been an attempt to bypass the difficult solutions of the identity crisis. It is of interest to note that these regressive symptoms had not occurred while both she and her future husband had been in graduate school together, maintaining their own separate homes and enjoyed a love affair which did not relieve them of the continuing work on their separate intra-psychic conflicts. It seemed as though the formalizing of the relation-ships, the "escape into marriage," was not a step toward maturity, as families and friends had thought, but an attempt to avoid the continu-ing responsibility for working on their individual identity problems.

3. *The end of role-playing*

The threat to the end of role-playing, which we had called another postadolescent characteristic, can be avoided temporarily by the escape-into-marriage move, which often turns out to be a specific form of role-playing: playing house. We should clearly distinguish this behavior from the typical adolescent sexual games and affairs, which are phase-specific activities. While the adolescent form of sexual behavior is also a form of role-playing, we may consider it *play-acting*, in contrast to the escape-into-marriage game, which is no longer play-acting, but *acting out*. Clinically, the difference is significant, as in all behavior which extends beyond the developmental phase.

A brief clarification of the two related concepts may help to dis-tinguish this aspect of adolescence from postadolescence.

To the extent to which we consider play-acting as representing be-havior in the service of future growth, heterosexual activities in ado-lescence may be considered a play solution, with partial reality testing, partially impulsive, partially ego directed.

If the adolescent ego is not hampered by early traumas, it would move from this point toward "delay and adaptive directions, with the increasing establishment of the secondary process, delay of impulsive discharge, increase of genuine object relationships,"[19] in brief, toward the possibility of marriage.

In the escape-into-marriage mechanism, on the other hand, we notice instead a regression to acting out, which is "a more primitive mode of attempted problem solving,"[19] an attempt to resolve conflicts of the past through a make-believe, role-playing solution, which is modeled after the original oedipal situation. Where the conflicts in healthy adolescence become more internalized by the maturing ego, they are externalized in acting out, in the attempt to extend the role-playing phase beyond its time. As in all acting out, which "in the analysis of adult neurotics is considered a substitute for recollection," the escape-into-marriage play is the kind of acting out which Ekstein and Fried-man defined as "a form of experimental recollection."[19]

What makes this form of acting out particularly complex and often refractory to therapeutic intervention is the fact that it is often unconsciously brought on by the original models: the parents are pressuring for marriage of the young people, offering to help in any way they can and, quite unconsciously, are further contributing toward the extension of the role-playing mechanism.

That some forms of acting out are "unconsciously fostered and sanctioned by the parents" has of course been pointed out many times, by Johnson, Szurek,[20] and many others. While these authors are referring mainly to antisocial acting out, the mechanism described is equally applicable to such socially acceptable forms of behavior as the escape into marriage.

The dynamics are basically the same: "the mother, because of structural defects in her own personality, does not allow the ego of the child to become an independently operating agency. Instead, her ego continues to act for him and to maintain direct contact with his id, or more properly with his id representatives, and in turn a situation is perpetuated in which his ego is directly influenced by her id representatives. Thus, instead of the child establishing within himself a structure that would allow conflicts to be worked out between his own ego and his own id, he remains in a state in which his ego continues to be fully susceptible to stimulation by the id of the mother."[21]

In the cases of two partners acting out together in the escape-into-marriage mechanism, we usually find at least one set of parents encouraging or furthering this behavior. The most characteristic way in which this support takes place is through economic means. At least one set of parents of the escape-into-marriage couple is likely to maintain their lifelong financial support, thus leaving the young couple in exactly the same economic state in which they had been in infancy, childhood and adolescence. By not being allowed to take financial responsibility for their marriage—a state which is known long before the mechanism is set in motion—the young couple has the illusion of financial independence without being anchored in reality. The house, the furniture and clothes all seem to be their own, but in reality godlike parental figures pay the bills and continue to exert the same influence that they have used in the past. The role-playing thus can continue through this escape-into-marriage game, since the young people are shielded against the full impact of reality and seldom get a chance to test reality from the vantage point of their own autonomous ego.

4. *Recognition of time continuity*

We had suggested in the discussion of this characteristic of post-adolescence that the fuller acceptance of the limitation of time is often accompanied by mild depressions or states of depersonalizations, because this recognition is experienced as a narcissistic injury, requiring a more definite cathexis of ego boundaries. Understandably, when the ego of the young adult is not sturdy enough to cope with this blow, he will attempt to return to the concept of a timeless, never-ending existence, a state of omnipotence, the oceanic feeling of Nirvana.

One of the many ways in which he can avoid the fuller recognition of the time continuity is the escape-into-marriage move, which creates for him and society the illusion that he has indeed made a very long-range plan, indicating that he has fully coped with the time continuity. Did he not agree to stay with his partner "until death do you part?" What could be more long-range than the marriage vow?

To label the young adult who takes this vow, as part of the escape-into-marriage mechanism, "insincere" or "irresponsible" would not help us to understand the improperly balanced ego state. So far as the young adult knows, he means what he says: This is for keeps, with no end in sight. If he has not been able really to make full contact with the time continuity, he cannot fathom as vast a concept as a lifetime any more than a small child can perceive as limited a time concept as next month or in four weeks. It has no real meaning until the secondary process is fully established, reality testing part of the adaptive action of the mature ego, and until all remnants of autism or temporary fantasy gratification have been given up.

Young adults in analysis are sometimes able to recognize the dynamics of the escape-into-marriage act, because they may have been able to discover for themselves some of the differences between fantasy and reality action. One young woman, who tended to act out many of her unresolved conflicts, began her analysis early in spring only to return to the couch after the analyst's summer vacation with the announcement that she and her friend had decided to get married. The announcement was made defensively, with references to her parents' broken marriage, the economic advantages of one household, the observation that "nothing was very different from before we went to the minister." When the analyst remained silent, the patient's anxiety increased, latent guilt was more openly verbalized with the significant statement that "if things don't work out we can always split."

There is in this association a partial awareness of both the role-playing, acting-out aspect of the escape into marriage, as well as the attempt to avoid the full impact of the time-continuity recognition. We are not discussing here the many other important aspects of this behavior, including the interesting transference manifestations, because the case was merely cited to illustrate one of the ways in which the time continuity may be temporarily avoided by formalizing an adolescent love relationship.

Another, not unusual, way in which the time concept is avoided is by fantasies about the power of time, as part of the escape-into-marriage behavior. Young adults frequently are ready to admit that their adolescent relationship had many problems, did not seem to lend itself to a permanent union, yet they often go ahead, in spite of all clear signs, acting out the escape into marriage. Therapists and leaders of youth who have had occasion to counsel young couples prior to marriage are familiar with the argument that "she will change in time" or "he will get over this in a few years of living with me." This sometimes moving and naive faith in time as an agent that can produce change is as much part of the avoidance of the time continuity as the inability to fully recognize it as a realistic measure of duration. The latter concept is rather like the ending of fairy tales, the traditional "and they lived happily ever after," an avoidance of the reality of time continuity which is appropriate for this form of literature.

Some young adults have expressed their misgivings about the escape into marriage after they had to recognize that this escape did not, after all, lead to a firmer grasp of reality or time continuity. They did come to the point in their venture where they had to recognize that it had been a mistake and attempted to undo it, only to discover that the undoing was much more difficult than the doing. One young woman suggested that it would be more helpful if getting married were made as difficult as getting divorced. She thought requirements and tests for marriage should be tough and difficult, not as easy as they were now. This request and criticism of our laws reflect the call for firmer ego-boundary substitutes by society for those young adults who use marriage as an escape from the end of role-playing and recognition of time continuity.

It was interesting to observe the role of the parents in divorce cases where the escape into marriage had in part been an acting out of the mother's id demands, as suggested in the discussion of role-playing. I have seen several cases where the same mother who had offered to help finance the marriage, the house, and the living expenses for the time being also offered to help with the divorce, with the trip to Mexico, the legal arrangements, the new living arrangements after the divorce. Both, the marriage and the divorce, were accepted with the same "objective" or "liberal" attitude that had prevailed all through the lives of the young people. By not experiencing the full impact of the beginning or the end of the escape into marriage, the postadolescent can further avoid the full recognition of time continuity, since in his experience time has played no part.

In summary, then, the difficult search for the partner in postadolescence is sometimes given up in favor of a pseudosolution, which we have called escape into marriage. This move may serve as a temporary shortcut for many of the unresolved postadolescent struggles. We took each of the postadolescent characteristics—aspects of the identity struggle, the self-image dilemma, the end of role-playing and recognition of time continuity—in an attempt to show how each of them could be temporarily bypassed by the escape into marriage. It could be called the fifth characteristic of postadolescence.

This concludes our discussion of the metapsychologic characteristics of postadolescence. They will now be supplemented by some of the sociologic factors in the following section of Part I. After the discussion of both the psychologic and sociologic aspects of postadolescence, we shall proceed to our application of this theoretical knowledge to clinical practice in Part II: Clinical Adaptations.

SOCIO-ECONOMIC FACTORS

5. The Economic Bind

THROUGHOUT THE PREVIOUS SECTION we have frequently referred to sociologic and economic factors as relevant aspects of postadolescence. In order to retain some order in the structure of the book, we had restricted ourselves to the discussion of metapsychologic factors and postponed the material on the social reality to this part.

For those clinicians who tend to pay no more attention to these factors than some social scientists do to intrapsychic aspects of behavior, we recall Waelder's statement on "Fundamental Concepts of Psychoanalysis":

"In the psychoanalytic view . . . thought and opinion are only in marginal cases determined by unconscious factors alone (as, e.g., in hallucinatory psychosis or in extreme cases of wishful thinking); usually thought and opinion are the result of an *interplay of forces,* some reflecting unconscious motives, others the impact of reality, with unconscious forces playing a greater or lesser role as the case may be."[22]

Of the many different forces which constitute the social reality of postadolescence, we have chosen some for discussion in this and the next few chapters. It seems appropriate to begin with a discussion of the "economic bind" of young adulthood, since his role in the marketplace has a very direct bearing on his self-image dilemma, his identity confusion, as well as on the other metapsychologic characteristics.

Basically, the economic bind results from the fact that young adults want to pay their own way, while our society not only makes no provision for their participation in the labor force, but actively keeps them out. Unlike youth in our colonial history or in partially industrialized countries, where young people are needed in the economy, young adults in this society are not wanted in the marketplace.

This is made abundantly evident by statements of economists, whether they speak from the viewpoint of management or labor.

"Where childhood is regarded as a national asset . . . youth . . . seems more and more to be regarded as a national problem like traffic congestion, water pollution or slums," says Charles E. Silberman in *Fortune,*[23] and he goes on to document his statement by pointing out that young people "who represent just 8% of the labor force account for 22% of total unemployment."

Under the title "Specter of Mass Youth Unemployment," the AFL-CIO spokesman puts it more strongly when he says in the *Federationist*[24] that "of 4 million people out of work in 1964 over 1.5 million were under 25 years of age. Though they make up less than 20% of the work force they accounted for more than 40% of national unemployment. The growing large scale unemployment has, according to former President of Harvard, James Conant, the makings of 'social dynamite.' Each year about 4 million will turn 18 years and one out of six youths between 16-20 was unemployed in 1964."

The prospects for the predictable future suggest that this state is not limited to this or next year, but represents a pattern of the economy, which must be taken into consideration in any realistic attempt to understand postadolescence.

Harold Taylor, the Director of the W. E. Upjohn Institute for Employment Research, details this pattern in his address before the National Industrial Conference Board, an address entitled "The Avalanche of Youth into the Labor Force."[25]

"The present year (1965) as far as the labor force is concerned can be termed the First Year of the Avalanche, which cannot possibly subside before 1982 . . . During the remaining years of the sixties, the number of new entrants to the labor force, largely because of these youngsters (!), will be 500,000 a year more than the number of new entrants that we were accustomed to only a few years ago."

He compares this avalanche of youth into the labor force with the overproduction of steel or oil and predicts unemployment "beyond comfortable levels" once we force ourselves to recognize the present situation as "involving an over-supply of labor." He sees hope in the fact that more and more young people stay in college and go on to graduate schools, thus delaying their "avalanche" into the labor force.

This is not only a telling comment on the role of education in our economy, it also serves to document the previous statement that young adults are not wanted in the marketplace. This open rejection by society comes at a point of the growth cycle when all healthy aspects of the young adult's self push for emotional and economic independence. For the majority of young adults in the lower and lower-middle economic classes, the identity crisis is heightened by this rejecting attitude of society. Since 22 per cent of the total unemployed come from postadolescents, it is harder, as Silverman points out in *Fortune*,[23] to achieve a feeling of identity "when unemployment justifies the feeling: I can't make it." He adds to this the pertinent fact that it now "takes 14 years of education to compete with machines."

But the complexity of the social reality for the postadolescent does not end with society's rejection of the young adult as an equal producer of values for the marketplace. It may seem contradictory at first sight, but it is a fact that while he is not wanted as a producer, he is highly valued and sought after as a consumer. In such articles as "How to Reach the College Market," the authors estimate a market worth $15 billion.[26] The knowledgeable *Wall Street Journal* suggests that the boom in young adults will help business, as most economists believe.[27]

The postadolescent then is a highly desirable target for the young adult market. He is being wooed by a large section of the economy, played up to by business, market research specialists, treated as though his culture were the most desirable development possible. Hipsterism is highly profitable to sections of business, and therefore it is being hailed by Madison Avenue, publicized and photographed, debated in the mass media and exploited for personal profit. It is an ironic comment on this state of young adulthood in our culture that a car manufacturer can sell more cars by calling them "Rebel." "Rebel" is "in," after having lost the meaning of "Sturm und Drang" or the impatient change from the status quo to a state in which youth can have an identity and a self-image.

This is, in essence, the core of the economic bind of postadolescence. The young adult is being prevented from making his own way economically, but is exploited as a consumer of luxury goods, for which he earns the money by part-time jobs, subsidies from home, school or government.

If we fully recognize the impact of this economic paradox, we can begin to understand if the young adult, in the midst of the identity crisis and the self-image dilemma, asks plaintively exactly what is reality. He asks this question earnestly, as part of the quest for identity, an attempt to orientate himself in the social reality.

While he has navigated through adolescence with the shaky economic basis of part-earning, part-allowance, dependence on home for room and board, guilt over asking for something and uncertainty over his right to make independent choices contrary to the wishes of those on whom he is economically dependent, there is the bright star of "Age 21," which is the legal cut-off point when he can be on his own. This characteristic aspect of postadolescence, instead of clarifying the problem of self and the object world, distorts the concept further because of the economic bind.

A young patient who had turned twenty-one in his third year of college described the inevitable complexity and confusion. Because living at home had been too difficult for the past two years, he had taken his own apartment for which he paid the rent himself from earnings in his father's store. However, all other expenses for living, education and recreation came from his father. He did not like to accept any money from his father—who had perpetuated their latent homosexual relationship with overwhelming gifts of money and objects—but faced the fact that working full time would have meant interrupting his education. Although he was not at all certain that he wanted the bachelor's degree, he stayed in school, partly to please his father, partly because of the realistic awareness that a college degree was the equivalent to a union card. Because of the previously described depersonalization aspects of the postadolescent identity crisis, the severe self-image dilemma and the psychosexual confusions—in his case aggravated by his father's unresolved problems—the young man had chosen a major without any particular conviction. If his college advisor had not pressed him, he would have been very willing to go on without choosing any major, to take courses, read the assigned books, write the assigned papers and pass the required tests. He had chosen philosophy as his major and was doing better than average work. The choice of philosophy also had been partly an attempt to please father, who took pleasure in telling his friends that his only son had gone back to the noble tradition of his talmudic heritage. When the young man was asked what he planned to do after college, he shrugged his shoulders and answered in a vague way.

There was a certain hopelessness and apathy in his voice when he explained his dilemma: He was interested in philosophy and perhaps teaching to some extent, but his interest in writing fiction seemed equally strong—neither promised a sound economic future for many years to come. He could always get "a job" in one of the advertising agencies where he had worked during summer vacations, but the salary was so small that he could never hope to support himself from it. In the background there was always the lure of his father's support, either through a job in father's business or by accepting further financial support from him. There did not seem any clear solution.

As he turned twenty-one, his father handed him five thousand dollars, the face value of an educational insurance policy which had matured at age twenty-one. It had been taken out in the son's name, but since father had financed the young man's education with other income, the money was now legally his to do with as he saw fit—with certain suggestions attached. Inasmuch as he did not need the money now—because father paid for all the essentials except the young man's apartment—it would be a good idea to invest this sum in real estate or a piece of land that promised to become valuable in the future. One of father's good friends, a real estate agent, was waiting for a call from the young man to discuss possible parcels of land. But, of course, everything was up to the young man himself. He was now of age!

We can understand it if the young adult asks, just what is reality?

"I'm more confused than ever" the young man said. "Nothing makes any sense at all. Here I'm in college, for which my father is paying, living in the apartment which I call "mine" but which I couldn't afford if my father would not support me otherwise . . . with no idea of where I'm going, with no clear prospect of ever earning a decent living—and now I'm supposed to call a real estate agent to buy some land! What business do I have buying anything—like a used car or a better stereo or land, of all things! It's my father's money, and we go on buying things for fun, making believe that we have the right to choose . . . sure I'm unsure, I take my girl out for dinner and put on the dog . . . that's okay if you're a kid of fifteen and your old man hands you a bill and says: 'Here, have a good time. You know it's not for real, but how about at twenty-one . . . isn't there supposed to be a difference? I don't know what's mine and what is somebody else's . . . this insurance money is just sitting there in the bank . . . I don't have the gall to spend it on stuff . . . but buying land seems ridiculous for a young guy like myself. I can't tell my father how I feel about it . . . he insists that it's mine. I just don't feel it is . . . if you've never earned enough to take care of yourself, money is more like the game of monopoly . . . it's not for real . . . even though I know up here that it is . . ."

This young adult is illustrating some of the ways in which the economic bind complicates the identity conflicts, the self-image dilemma, the approach to the end of role-playing. The particular socioeconomic situation encourages further role-playing, rather than enabling him to give it up; it prevents further separation from the incestuous love objects, making autonomy development more difficult; it keeps the precarious self-image balance in the most labile state, making it nearly impossible for him to side with the superego or the ego-ideal in his choice of a profession that would leave him a conflict-free, realistic solution.

After remaining in this state for another two years, this young adult chose the previously discussed escape-into-marriage solution, reasoning that once he was married he would have to make up his mind about a job and the necessity of supporting his wife. He took this step with the greatest misgivings but was convinced that without it he would just go on remaining a student "forever," living off his father and never being "on my own."

He felt that he could not get the status of an adult citizen without being a "family man," who would have to be taken seriously in the

marketplace, like any other working man. As long as he was single, he
felt that he was part of his father's family and had no right to demand a
living wage or job security, tenure and profit-sharing. With the legal
claim of having to support a wife—and perhaps even a child in the near
future—he could talk and act like any other man. With a wedding ring
on his finger, a homemade lunch under his arm, a budget to live by, he
felt he was "somebody." For him the marital status was a substitute for
his unresolved identity confusion, his self-image dilemma. Although
the relationship was not satisfactory, he clung to it as long as possible,
because he felt that being married was the only way in which he could
get over feeling "like a kid."

Unlike other young adults who continue "playing house," with one
or both parents continuing their lifelong support, this young man took
the opposite position and refused any kind of help from home, even
where it would have been reasonable on a temporary or loan basis.
Clearly, he continued the polarized conformity-opposition attitude
which is most characteristic for the middle phase of adolescence. He
was apparently so caught up in the economic bind that he was unable
to arrive at any truly conflict-free, autonomous ego balance which
should have enabled him to make flexible, rational choices, appropriate
to the situation at the time.

That the economic bind had become so central in his thinking, is of
course related to the ego development throughout his life up to this
point. As we suggested in the beginning of this chapter, we are always
confronted with the interplay of forces, some reflecting unconscious
motives, others the impact of reality, but there seems little doubt about
the fact that the economic bind in postadolescence hampers the most
fortuitous development of the ego at this phase of the lifecycle.

For the lower-class young adult who has not had the opportunity to
develop all his potential intellectual and cultural resources, the only
concrete way that seems to spell "independence" in his mind is to quit
school and get "a job." He may quit in high school or in the early
years of college, but if he is intensely troubled by the identity crisis, the
self-image dilemma and the pressures from home to "do something," he
will insist on embarking on the road that leads to the marketplace. As
the figures, quoted earlier in this chapter, show, he will become part of
the mass of unemployed youth, which comprises nearly half of the total
unemployment in our economy. If this is true in a period of relative
economic stability, it is not difficult to see the impact of the economic
bind on postadolescence in a time of economic crisis or mass unemployment.

There is neither an official recognition—aside from some federal
stop-gap programs—nor the status attached to other discriminated

minority groups in this country, but there is no doubt about the fact that there is economic discrimination against the young adult in our society. This is particularly valid for the post-adolescent who for many different reasons has left his assigned place in the protected shelter of school or college and ventured out into the mainstream of the economy, unprepared, ill-equipped and destined to take his place instead at the fringe of society.

Unlike his peers from middle and upper-middle class background with high upward mobility, the young adult from the lower class or one of the discriminated minorities knows that he is caught in the economic bind. For him the economic bind of postadolescence becomes a more or less permanent state. He is realistically discouraged and sees no point in growing up. Postadolescence and the economic bind therefore become a way of life for a substantial share of young adults in our culture.

6. Group Formation and Social Isolation

THE SOCIAL ASPECTS of the economic bind in postadolescence constitute still another characteristic of this phase of growth, as differentiated from earlier phases. The most prominent manifestations are the formation, the climate and the functioning of groups at this level of development.

It is axiomatic that the group as the "nursery of human nature in the world about us," as Cooley phrased it half a century ago,[28] changes its function with the development of the ego, with all this adaptive process implies. Just before postadolescence, the group represented a source of protection for the adolescent against the adult world, but even within this camp the socioeconomic structure of the adult society had made a definite and measurable impact. This was perhaps most clearly demonstrated by Hollingshead in his classical study of *Elmtown's Youth*,[29] in which he related the "observed behavior of adolescents to the positions that their families occupied in the social structure of the community." Clique membership and dating was primarily composed of students in the same school and "prestige class or adjacent ones."

If we relate this behavior to the characteristic adolescent struggle against the authority of the family—a turning away from the source of the reawakened drive conflicts—we notice the beginning of the identity diffusion and the self-image dilemma: while the adolescent struggles for autonomy and faces the superego versus ego-ideal conflict, he typically patterns his friendship choices and dating behavior after the position that his family occupies in the community. In spite of brief flurries into associations with members of distant classes, he characteristically stays close to the socioeconomic level of his own rejected family.

This paradox presents a challenge to the leadership of adolescent groups, as emphasized by Redl[30] and others. By applying the method of role-playing to the leadership function, Redl arrives at ten types of group formation, conceptually distinguished by the role of the central person: as an object of identification, as an object of drives, or as ego support.

The seeming contradiction between the rebelling and the conforming adolescent is also relevant to the clinician for a better understanding of the formation of the identity diffusion and the self-image dilemma, as we pointed out when discussing reference groups in connection with the superego, ego-ideal conflict.

The significant difference in the function of the group in adolescence as distinguished from postadolescence may lie in the fact that the protective role of group formation diminishes in young adulthood, while the recognition of time continuity and the end of role-playing require increasingly permanent alignments along social, political, religious lines.

As identification is replaced by identity in social group behavior, the choice of objects, individual and group, is less determined by the leader of a group or even the activity of a group to the degree to which they can aid in the resolution of the self-image dilemma.

We had suggested that in postadolescence the group typically represents the collective personification of the young adult's ego-ideal, while in earlier adolescence the group and the leader can still be used for identification. When a postadolescent patient tells me that he does not want to be "bracketed" with this social or political group, he gives me some indication of his ego-ideal or superego alignment. This kind of statement would not be made by a young man at the earlier phases of adolescence, who would be more concerned with the activity of the group or whether he liked the boys or girls in the club.

A young man in his last year of college, for example, became quite suddenly very active in a protest movement on his campus. The organization had been formed to protest a rise in tuition. The patient, like most of the members of the group, did not pay the tuition himself and had never been very concerned about his parents' educational expenses. He readily admitted that he did not have particularly strong feelings about the slight rise in tuition, but had wanted to join a protest group, because he liked the idea of being considered a rebel, a fighter for causes, rather than the conforming, excellent student that he had been known as. He had scorned the conventional protest symbols through adolescence—long hair, a beard, smoking "pot," or staying up all night—but he had searched for some anti-establishment group whose goals he could accept. He had participated in some civil rights activities, but more on an individual than a group basis, traveling south with a friend to help with voter registration and teaching underprivileged children. As a strong believer in public education, with a desire to be able to pay his own tuition or get a free education, the idea of a rise in tuition was a sufficient motivation for him to join—for the first time in his college life—an existing, active group.

The group came closest to his ego-ideal, while his role as a serious, hard-working, but conforming student expressed the superego of the self-image dilemma. The way he became involved in the group illustrates some of the aspects of his dilemma.

Drifting into one of the large meeting halls one evening, he found himself standing near the platform, listening to the leading speaker making an impassioned plea for the lowering of tuition, scholarships for gifted students, state and federal aid. The patient broke into spontaneous applause which was taken up by many other students. When the speaker asked for audience reactions, the young man jumped up on the platform, seized the microphone and began to talk quite spontaneously. Since he spoke with eloquence and reason, the large group responded to him and made him feel at home in a situation which he usually would not have been involved in. Although he, himself, was bewildered by his behavior, he liked being asked to take some leading positions in the organization, later that week, and then found himself deeply entrenched in a major political battle, which went beyond the tuition issue and led to some prominence for him.

When his family and some older friends presented him with the issue of the newspaper in which his photo figured, together with a militant headline, he experienced the self-image dilemma acutely. He had to confront an image of himself which represented his ego-ideal, while the superego aspect of himself was kept in abeyance, but not sufficiently to avoid some weeks of doubt and long nights of discussion, during which the two different ego ideals were actively battling each other.

The existence of the group, which was now his reference group, represented the collective personification of the ego-ideal. That it was a group, rather than an individual authority, determined his choice at that time.

Where the superego had been too punitive or powerful, preventing the ego from expanding, the group in postadolescence often becomes a necessary ally of the ego-ideal in the struggle against the inner censorship. Social psychologists have long pointed out that "the coming together in informal associations provides a . . . strong motivational basis which is not effectively fulfilled by young people themselves as individuals."[31] The reference group now serves as the theatre of operation in which the battle of the self-image dilemma can be enacted. While "the interaction among the individuals over a period of time becomes the source of satisfaction and frustration . . . ,"[31] the superego representatives may intrude and affect the group behavior.

A young medical student who, like the young man mentioned above, had cast about for a suitable group affiliation found a notice on the bulletin board announcing the formation of a union of graduate students in the university. The basis of the organization appealed to her, since the status of graduate student represented the ego-ideal aspect of the self-image dilemma. She went to a few meetings and joined the new group. Since she had been in analysis at the time, some of her feelings about having joined were spontaneously expressed, illustrating the dilemma:

"Only one other medical student in the group . . . most of the people are history and English majors . . . my neighbor from our dorm, who is the other member from the medical school, joined only because her boy friend is one of the founders. I'm kind of alone as somebody who joined purely as a graduate student. They asked us to sign a petition to the president, asking for smaller classes and more time for independent research. I signed it but I'll feel funny if the dean of our school sees my name on it . . . I like him and he has helped me quite a bit. Besides, I don't need more time for independent research . . . that may be true for history people . . ."

What concerned her was the reaction of the dean, who represented the role of a protecting, stern father. The patient had some difficulties in some of her subjects and felt that without the guiding hand of the dean she might not be able to stay in graduate school. At the same time she wanted to break out of the isolation position in which she had been most of her adolescent and graduate-school life. Because of the particular nature of her ambivalent strivings, this young woman handled her self-image dilemma in the same way in which she did all her basic conflicts: she stayed in the group, became the opposition leader and attempted to make the members conform more toward her superego demands—while in her talks with the dean she took every opportunity to emphasize the just demands of the group "which I hope to make more realistic." (It is of passing interest here—where the topic is group formation—that the patient behaved in the same way with her boy friend, a younger and less accomplished, but less troubled young man. To the extent to which he was brash, demanding, spontaneous, she identified with him, since this—as the group—represented part of her ego-ideal, while on the other side, she tried to reform him, get him to finish college and to pay for his own apartment.)

But there was a more basic reason that made this young woman remain in the group, in spite of some of her misgivings: the fear of permanent social isolation.

This awareness of permanent social isolation is another characteristic of postadolescence, connected with the end of role-playing and the recognition of time continuity.

Those young adults—as the young medical student—who have never been very popular with either individuals or groups, in childhood or adolescence, now experience the familiar social "Angst," the dread that the earlier hopes of a change in their social status were unrealistic. As they vascillate from states of depersonalization to realistic self-aware-ness, they also review their relative isolation position in all previous groups and come to recognize that this is going to be a permanent role in their adult life ahead.

To many young adults this seems to be their last chance for a solid social affiliation, to belong to a group of people in which they can be at home, where they are liked and respected and where what they have to say counts for something. This fear of permanent social isolation persists, independent of the existence of personal relationships. The young medical student had her boy friend and one or two girl friends, but she felt keenly her social isolation, a position familiar to her throughout her whole life.

She had neither the continuity of the family group—which often serves as a substitute for autonomous social group affiliations in post-adolescence and in adulthood—nor the church or a highly motivated interest group in which she could feel comfortably entrenched. How-ever, until this point she had not been as fully aware of the isolated position in which she found herself.

Like the young man who found himself involved in the battle against higher tuition, this patient too had found a social harbor which served her need to be part of a meaningful social unit. In spite of all the objections, both young people expressed in their individual ways the idea that "some group is better than no group at all."

While the increasingly meaningful research by group-dynamic workers helps us to understand this need,[32] we, who work clinically with the individual member of the group, are particularly interested in the factors that determined the choice of this, rather than that group.

The young medical student could have joined a number of other groups besides the union of graduate students. She could have been active in the alumni association of her college; she could have been a respected member of the university glee club, whose weekly rehearsals she attended; she could have participated in several of the civil rights groups to whom she contributed some money and in which she might be expected to have some interest since her boy friend was Negro and himself active in one of the large civil rights organizations.

What determined her choice of the union of graduate students as her reference group, over all the other potential group affiliations, which could have served as outlets for the need to register protest, to be pop-ular, to contribute to community causes? By referring to "status" we are not indicating more than that this group represented her ego-ideals as we had pointed out before, but we have so far failed to discover what makes this group more eligible as an ego-ideal representative than the other potential groups.

From the knowledge of this patient, it would seem reasonable to state that this group was cathected with more libido than any other group, because it paid the greatest dividends in narcissistic gratifications. Brought up by a near-psychotic mother, whose hostility had been introjected into the early ego, barely saved from schizophrenia by a more benign but completely unreliable father, who left the home when the patient was five years old, this young woman was so fundamentally uncertain about the reality of her existence as an autonomous organism that she was never able to believe any of her hard-won accomplishments, from elementary school through college. If a stranger would learn that she was a graduate student and jestingly doubted it, because she looked so very young, the patient would shortly begin to doubt the reality of her being a graduate student. This professional accomplishment was her highest achievement and was made more real by the existence of a group in which one had to be a graduate student to belong.

That this state in her development was highly cathected with libido for her and could be used as ego-ideal representation, points to the nature of her narcissism. In distinguishing between healthy and pathologic narcissism, Federn[33] made some observation pertinent to our discussion of group formation. After emphasizing that the concept of "narcissism" should not be restricted to the realm of pathology, he defines healthy narcissism as "counter-cathexis to the object-strivings and for their support, but not as their substitute. The more narcissism functions as such a substitute, the more pathological it becomes."

From the few remarks about the patient we already recognize that her ego boundaries are not very resistant, that she tends to merge with objects very rapidly. Dependent on the objects, the young woman would feel connected or isolated and suffer from almost constant anxiety.

The reference group that she chose provided her ego boundaries with a strong narcissistic cathexis. Federn suggests that "ego boundaries, expanded to a common identification, may obtain an extremely strong narcissistic cathexis without prejudice to the simultaneous continuation of the individual ego boundary—for example, in nationalism, in religious or political associations or in military units—and through their resistance, provide the individuals with a much desired strong support."

If we understand the nature of the ego and their boundaries, if we have a clear picture of the narcissistic countercathexis and the way this affects the particular aspects of identity and the self-image dilemma in postadolescence, we could think of characteriologic classifications in relation to choice of groups and particular group formations.

While it is not the purpose of this book to develop such a systematic classification, we can make some observations about group formation and social isolation, based on an informal survey of some fifty young adults, most of whom had been patients, while a smaller percentage had been studied in nonclinical relationships.

THE ISOLATES

Ten of the fifty young people can be described as social isolates, by which we mean that they had never been deeply involved in groups comprising more than two other people. They all had formed face-to-face relationships with one other person. This behavior did not seem directly related to their position in the primary group, the family. Two of the ten were only children, two were older siblings, two were middle children, one was the third of four children, two were youngest children, one grew up with two stepsisters from her father's former marriage.

All of them had been exposed to play groups in kindergarten, to interest groups in latency (such as boy or girl scouts), to activity groups in early adolescence (basketball, dramatics, orchestra). They had participated in the activities without becoming involved in interpersonal relationships.

There were no common denominators in regard to sex, race or religion, social class or cultural influences. Intelligence ranged from normal to superior, performance in high school or college varied from average to excellent.

Clinically, however, they could all be classified in the so-called "borderline" category. While this label is not descriptive, as Knight has pointed out,[34] we are referring to it here to suggest some degree of autistic thinking, observable in the Rorschach, degrees of inappropriate affect, occasional breaks in reality testing, some peculiarities or bizarreness in behavior which they had sensed early and to which they reacted by withdrawal from intensive social contact.

In postadolescence, all of them found for themselves a particular social function, which allowed them to continue their isolate status, while at the same time giving them a loose connection with a group. One young woman, for example, took on the job of secretary of her high school alumni group as the high school affiliations drew to a close.

In this role she did not need to relate to any one member of the alumni, but by keeping records and sending out occasional notices, she appeased the superego aspect of her self-image, which demanded in her culture that one had a definite function in a group.

One young man became the self-appointed business manager of a traveling jazz band, which did not require direct participation in the group but allowed him to make his individual contacts with night-clubs or record companies, where he could perform a useful function for the group without being centrally involved with the active members.

Another young isolate who was concerned about civil rights did not join one of the large national or local organizations, but made posters and left pamphlets in conspicuous places of her small-town college, where no chapter of any national organization existed. When a few of the students showed interest in her pamphlets, she did not take any leadership herself but got one of the more popular students to take the lead and form a small group on the campus. Once this group was formed, the young woman functioned as a silent partner in the background without being directly involved.

In a similar vein, the other young people in the isolate category seemed to have made a realistic adaptation to the superego demands, without altering the restrictive ego limitations. It seems to be one of their defenses against more definite isolation, loneliness or depression. Unless they chose therapy to work through the fears of involvement, this solution seems to be a realistic compromise.

Members of Groups

Except for the ten young people whom one could describe as social isolates, the other young people in this small sample belonged to some group, in different capacities. Like the isolates, they too came from a wide variety of social and economic backgrounds, represented no pattern in choice of interest, ability or pathology. Likewise, their ordinal positions in the family groups showed no common denominators.

All of them had belonged to play groups, activity and interest groups, but unlike the social isolates, had formed personal relationships along with their interest in the activities of the group. It was possible to discern several distinct friendship patterns, which had grown out of their activity groups, so that any one of the young people would have camp friends, glee-club friends, high-school-newspaper friends. These friendship circles sometimes overlapped, at other times were kept separate. In many instances the friendships continued beyond adolescence into adulthood.

As they moved into postadolescence, the nature of the group formation changed, together with the metapsychologic changes, as suggested earlier in this chapter. We had developed the idea that in postadolescence the group typically represents the collective personification of the young adult's ego-ideal and we had attempted to show some of the reasons why one group was chosen out of many possible ones.

Based on the sample of some forty young people who did participate in such groups, we find that those young people who had been active and formed interpersonal relationships in their groups through adolescence remained active in the young adult groups, but with very different motivations. Depending on the particular nature of the identity diffusion, the mode of their ambivalence, the compromises reached in the self-image dilemma, groups were chosen to support ego-syntonic goals of this phase of growth.

Socio-psychologic pressures, economic considerations, recognition of the end of role-playing were found to be highly significant in the motivations for belonging and participating in groups in postadolescence.

This is no longer the same correlation between social behavior and economic class, as described (and referred to earlier) by Hollingshead, who showed the observable behavior of adolescence related to the positions their families occupied in the social structure of the community.

Several distinct patterns of group formation could be distinguished. One of the most typical forms resembled the guild or the trade union, formed to promote professional and economic interests of the members. The time spent on discussions of a constitution or amendments suggested the members' preoccupation with the structure of the group, as well as the concern with the exclusive nature of the membership. Where these groups had community or national reputations, the membership represented "status" which could be translated as another collective personification of the ego-ideal. Unlike "in-groups" in adolescence—as, for example, hostile street gangs—these groups were concerned with increasing membership, as long as each individual had the credentials for belonging. As long as applicants agreed with the explicitly stated purposes of the organization, they were accepted, regardless of social or economic status, race or religion.

Another characteristic type of group formation was based on social action, as a broad and binding common interest. Unlike the "guild" form of group, these groups were informal in their organizational structure, fluid in membership, inclusive rather than exclusive, co-operative rather than competitive in their group climate. While the nature of the social action was frequently a protest against status quo, conditions on the local, national or international level, it sometimes took the form of social service, such as orienting new students to the campus or integrating foreign students into the community.

Unlike the adolescent rebel groups, in which the common interest is based on the need to express negativism or discharge hostility through as powerful and organizational a body as possible, the young adult's social action groups represent a more homogeneous structure which in many of the young people studied in this sample, has been used toward resolution of self-image dilemma and identity struggles. With the clear emphasis on social change, the individual in these groups exercises one of the basic ego functions, as Freud had detailed them in the *Outline*.[35] "As regards external events . . . the ego performs the task of self-preservation by learning to bring about appropriate modifications in the external world to its own advantage (through activity)."

For the young adult in particular, modifications in the external world require concern with social and political issues. Reality testing now includes a distinction between those aspects of the society which are in his self-interest and those which are clearly directed against it. The economic bind becomes an integral part of this social fabric against which young adults' social action groups have to be understood.

Finally, the young adult, more than the adolescent or the adult, carves within these action groups his social philosophy, lines it up against his moral and ethical conviction, and then states, as a member of such a group did, that "we have a certain relation to moral action, which is an integral part of our identity, both communally and personally."

This statement opens the way for discussing the integrating process of both metapsychologic and socio-economic processes: the "Weltanschauung."

7. Toward a "Weltanschauung"

THE GRADUAL EVOLUTION of a "Weltanschauung," a conception of events in the world leading to a philosophy of life, is another characteristic of young adulthood. The crystallization of an ideology during this phase of the life cycle proceeds at an uneven pace and at different levels of psychic growth. The flowering of an autonomous ideology, determination of his own personal values and ethical standards, is as much part of the Weltanschauung as formation of social or political opinions. All of it is part of the tapestry of the dignity, the self-respect and the sanctity of the individual in his society, a tapestry woven from his identity and his self-image, his adaptation to the reality which must include the social and economic life of his world and his time.

The constancy of the Weltanschauung of the young adult will have to depend on the degree to which he has been able to resolve some or all of the inner and outer conflicts that we have attempted to detail in the previous chapters.

When our postadolescent patients—usually early in treatment—present to us their Weltanschauung in the form of moral, political or ethical pronouncements, we can often gain valuable insights into the degree to which either id or superego have infiltrated the mediating role of the ego. It is helpful to remain aware of the fact that the emanation and flowering of a philosophy of life is a continual process, which goes on throughout life. Id and superego "may exercise their influence on the philosophy of adults, and even color their scientific convictions."[36]

If we consider the multitude of postadolescent characteristics both inside and outside the young adult, we can begin to fathom the difficulties any young man or young woman has in steering a fairly consistent course toward forming a realistic and functional philosophy of life.

We had suggested five metapsychologic characteristics of this phase of development:

The self-image crisis, in particular the conflict between the superego and differing ego-ideals.

Certain aspects of the identity struggle, in particular states of depersonalization and psychosexual identity diffusions.

The end of role-playing, in particular the sudden necessity to take on a permanent role that can no longer be changed at will.

The cognition of time continuity, in particular the necessity to make long-term commitments.

The search for the partner, in particular the inability to make conflict-free choices, which often leads to the escape into marriage.

We had also suggested two large areas of social and economic characteristics:

The economic bind, in particular, the young adult's need for economic independence and society's rejection of him as a producer, while he is highly valuable as a consumer of luxury goods.

Group-formation and social isolation, in particular the need for a reference group which represents the collective ego-ideal, partially to meet the realistic adult needs, partially to avoid social isolation.

If we add to these demands made on the ego of the young adult the socio-psychologic pressures in his culture, we can begin to consider the particular difficulties inherent in evolving a consistent Weltanschauung.

Whether he is ready for it or not, the young adult is now called upon to take his place in the society that he had considered until now the concern of the authorities of the past. Whatever the state of his ego at this juncture of his life, he is asked to vote, to serve in the armed forces, to go to war if this is the situation at the time, to take a stand for or against segregation, civil rights, civil liberties. His opinions are taken seriously, his advice is asked, his actions affect others.

These expectations and pressures from the outside world will have a share in finalizing the Weltanschauung of the young adult, who is still struggling with the inner conflicts that await resolutions.

The Weltanschauung that is now crystallizing represents a hierarchy of values, based in its native state on the total heritage, but more importantly, it is structured by the characteristics of postadolescence. If we relate the predominance of the various metapsychologic characteristics to the socio-economic ones, we get a more complex picture of the manner in which the young adult forms his Weltanschauung, makes his adaptation to reality.

The economic bind, for example, may seriously interfere with the resolution of the self-image dilemma; the social isolation may hasten the search for the partner or prolong the end of role-playing. In brief, we can visualize a great number of permutations of the various postadolescent characteristics, all of which have a direct connection to the formation of a Weltanschauung.

Hartmann suggested that "social value-systems are just like any other conventions (in the broadest sense of the word): though they often hinder adaptation, under certain conditions they can also facilitate it."[37]

The ego is attempting to integrate the social value systems with the hierarchy of ego-syntonic values inside the young adult, thus setting up a rank order of what will be considered "important" for the future adult life. In discussing the hierarchies of values, Hartmann suggests that some may be "directly hostile, others neutral to society, and some will contain social factors of the highest significance, as, for example, the valuation of the love for fellow men." He quotes Freud who wrote to Romain Rolland: "Given our drive disposition and our environment, the love for fellow men must be considered just as indispensable for the survival of mankind as is technology."[37]

While the "adoption of ethical value hierarchies may be (but need not) be useful for individual adaptation," Hartmann makes the connection to the problem of Weltanschauung when he suggests that "we will be more impressed with the usefulness of these value hierarchies if we take into account their role in the maintenance of society (or certain kinds of society)."

This is the area in which the young adult finds his greatest difficulties: the consideration of his individual needs within the contradictions of the society for which he is becoming increasingly responsible. One young adult who was seriously struggling with his value system in the pursuit of an ethical imperative while he was at the same time being groomed for an executive position in his father's business, asked with a wry smile, "How do you love thy neighbor on Sunday and beat your competitor the rest of the week?"

The young man was ridiculed for his naive question, just as truth-seekers have always been in history. If they did more than ask questions, if they did seriously interfere with what we now call "the establishment," they may be as much in danger of their existence as the men in the last sentence of Plato's cave allegory of whom he said: "If they could lay hands on such a man . . . they would kill him." As Hannah Arendt suggests in her essay "Truth and Politics,"[38] "the Platonic conflict between truth-teller and citizen cannot be explained by the Latin adage (*Fiat veritas* [*justitia*], *et pereat mundus*) or any of the later theories, that explicitly or implicitly, justify lying, among other transgressions, if the survival of the world is at stake." But whether this young adult has studied Hobbes and his indifferent truth, such as mathematical truth or Leibnitz in modern times, he will attempt to reconcile these basic contradictions in his search for a Weltanschauung. The more seriously he has taken such abstractions as freedom of political expression—as the protesting students have done in some large universities—the more difficult it will be for him to resolve the internal

conflicts that we have described before. The student who has been
nursed by his alma mater and who is evolving his personal view of the
world in which he will live his personal life, has always reacted with
characteristic behavior to the basic conflicts of individual and society.
Whether we call it "Sturm und Drang" or "Silent Generation,"
whether one considers the leadership of students in revolutions, the
young adult, with all his characteristics, is fighting with himself and
his environment for a Weltanschauung that permits him to achieve "a
better functioning synthesis and relation to the environment."[37]

It is of interest to recall that this statement by Hartmann is also a
definition of the aims of psychoanalytic therapy, which becomes necessary for an increasing number of young adults at this time of history.

Although exact figures are difficult to obtain, because a great many
services to young adults are not counted statistically, a recent publica-
tion[39] suggests that ten percent of all students will have emotional conflicts of sufficient severity to warrant professional help (1000 out of
every 10,000). Dr. Farnsworth of the Harvard Health Services suggests in his recent book that their services are available to 28,000 persons, including faculty members. The number of students who used
the services in this one college rose to 148,000 in 1966 from 117,000 in
1965. The presenting complaints were depression, apathy, sexual difficulties, in addition to severe learning impairments.

It would seem reasonable to assume that this number of patients who
will get brief services represents only a fraction of the large group of
young adults who are in trouble, to a minor or major degree. In addition to the student population, we do have the large army of young
people on unemployment and in industry who, as in the adult population, function on a marginal level without ever having had the
strength to face their own problems.

All of them are searching for a Weltanschauung, a way of life that is
good for them. Some of them are succeeding and articulate about the
interferences in their growth. It is of interest to clinicians in this connection to realize that concern with identity and depersonalization is
not limited to our profession.

The leader of one of the protest movements in one of the large universities refers to both these characteristics as interferences when he
writes: ". . . what struck me most about these young people thoroughly involved in this movement: that, confronting an institutional
entity apparently and frustratingly designed to *depersonalize* and block
communication, they found flowering in themselves the presence whose
absence they were in part protesting, for the beginning and end of my
(and I think our) concern is the individual. We have a certain relation

to moral action which is an integral part of our *identity,* both communally and personally . . ."

To the extent to which increasing depersonalization is becoming part of our culture, we should expect both more protest movements and more pathologic breakdowns. As clinicians we will have to be prepared to cope with the increasing load of disturbed postadolescents. As the director of the Harvard Health Services pointed out in his book,[39] a great many universities are offering clinical services, mainly of brief service nature. That these services can be very effective has been described and documented in the literature, particularly by Bellak.[40] He also makes very clear the limitations of emergency services and brief psychotherapy, and emphasizes the need for trained clinicians equipped to deal analytically with postadolescents. The second part of the book is written for them.

PART II: Clinical Adaptations

Introduction

IF THE CHARACTERISTICS of postadolescence are valid, we can assume that the young adult between the late teens and early twenties presents a particular situation for the clinician: some of the variations or modifications in technique suggested for adolescence and for child analysis[41] may still have validity, with particular consideration of the characteristics of postadolescence. There are also young adult patients who may be regarded and treated as adult patients.

Before we can discuss the many implications of this complex situation, we should first get the one question out of the way which is frequently asked and discussed among clinicians: Can the postadolescent be analyzed?

Since there is no definite consensus on this issue—for many reasons, most of them related to the *Schools of Analytic Thought*[42]—I can speak only for myself and share my own experience for whatever it may be worth. Over a period of twenty years I have treated nearly one hundred young adults, of which ten have had a full, classical, four-times-a-week analysis. The majority have been in psychoanalytic psychotherapy, a term which I hope to clarify throughout this section. Without having attempted a systematic investigation among colleagues, it would appear that my own experience seems to be similar to those clinicians who have worked extensively with young adults: About 10 per cent of their postadolescents could establish a transference, develop a transference neurosis, and resolve the transference.

However, it is significant to note that the ten young adults who had a full analysis started with a preparatory period during which they had an educational experience which then enabled them to tolerate the work of a full analysis.

This preparatory period differs in length from a few months to as much as a year and a half, approximately eight to eighteen months. This is quite frankly a learning situation, not to be confused with the somewhat limited analytic experience which the majority of young adult patients seem to have. This differentiation requires an early diagnostic commitment during the initial exploratory experience: We attempt to decide during this first consultation stage whether the postadolescent patient seems to be a patient for full analysis or whether we limit our goals from the start.

These basic considerations suggest a number of topics and their order to be discussed in the following pages:

We are starting with those issues that apply to all postadolescent patients, regardless of the kind of therapy which we decide on. Before we can see any of our young adult patients, they will have to be referred to us and called for an appointment. I have called this preliminary situation *"The Referral Triangle,"* which will be the first chapter in this section.

Once they are in our waiting room the *"Initial Consultation"* begins, our second chapter. During this diagnostic experience we will most typically arrive at the decision to proceed with a two-times weekly analytic therapy, instead of a full analysis. This will not be what Glover has called a "pseudo-analytical suggestion"[43] experience, but a limited psychoanalysis, with some *"Variations in Technique,"* determined by the postadolescent characteristics. This will be a brief theoretic discussion about the reasons for modifications in technique. A number of key issues will then be taken up in this order: *Transference and Countertransference"* in postadolescent patients, to be followed by *"Styles of Free Association"* which seem significant at this phase of growth. Moving from patient to therapist we are considering our own language in *"On Intervention and Interpretation."* Since the sociopsychologic characteristics such as the economic bind presents certain *"Special Technical Problems,"* we are going to discuss fee, bills, vacation, make-up policy in this chapter.

The section will close with the previously mentioned *"Education for Analysis"* for the small group of young adults who are intact enough to tolerate a complete analytic experience.

8. The Referral Triangle

WE KNOW FROM therapeutic work with adolescents that the referral of the patient to the therapist by a third party constitutes a triangle of interaction. The interplay between the three parties—both their conscious and unconscious motivations—is significant for the understanding of the transference. Since this interplay is set in motion frequently before the treatment process has begun, we pay particular attention to the very first telephone contact by a referring party. Often the adolescent patient identifies the referral party with the therapist, particularly since the family or school tends to interpret the function of therapy to the patient. Wherever possible we attempt to structure the interpretation of therapy independently from the referral party. The family, agency, or school which refers the adolescent patient often attempts to be helpful by offering diagnostic clues; at other times a parent may inadvertently announce his hoped-for goals of therapy—all of which has an effect on the adolescent patient and his expectations of therapy. Not infrequently the parent is the one who really asks for help for himself, sending the adolescent patient to be "adjusted" in order to relieve the familial distress. Conflicts in the family sometimes are used to influence the adolescent patient's attitude toward therapy—for or against—depending on the feuding factions in the family.

All of this operates to some degree also with postadolescent patients, with the additional complication that the role of the referral party is not as overt and directly visible as in adolescence or childhood.

Unlike the adolescent patient, the young adult usually makes his first contact with the therapist directly. But like the adolescent patient, the postadolescent too does not pay completely for his therapy himself, but has to obtain the consent of family or friends before he can begin treatment. The economic bind, one of the postadolescent characteristics, influences the patient-therapist relationship from the start. This constellation can affect the transference, quite in the same way as with adolescent patients, unless the therapist insists on a clear separation between his young adult patient and his family, or whatever the source of his financial support. Even where the young adult has nominal control of income—as in cases of inheritance or savings from part-time work—the actual economic dependence is frequently used by the patient as resistance.

Where the end of role-playing is combined with the economic bind, it is particularly necessary for the therapist to resist the invasion of family or other referral sources, to avoid being drawn into the referral triangle.

While family or relatives of child or adolescent patients frequently make the first contact with the therapist and attempt to direct the treatment relationship by open suggestions or questions, the referring source in young adult patients usually remains in the background and emerges openly only when the postadolescent patient asks for interference—usually as part of his resistance or acting out of negative transference phases.

A young college student who experienced brief states of depersonalization as part of his identity crisis while studying in his parents' home threatened to quit college and work full time, unless the family assisted him with his own apartment. Since this crisis followed an earlier one in which he had lived in a dormitory out of town, as part of the college setup, the family was anxious that he continue in this second school in his home town and agreed to pay for his maintenance as long as he would be willing to pay his own rent. The family, which had agreed to the choice of the young adult's therapist, paid for most of the treatment, while the young adult took responsibility for the remainder. When his acting out took the form of missing sessions, the family suddenly entered the picture, clearly summoned by the patient. While the therapist had made it clear to patient and family in an early telephone contact that the relationship would have to be strictly confidential and include only the patient and the therapist, the young man had now been using the financial contribution of his family in behalf of his resistance. By letting his family know that he had been missing sessions, he invited them to enter the triangle. The symptom of oversleeping, coming late for sessions, and missing sessions entirely had been one of his acting-out episodes which effectively blocked analysis of the transference. In an earlier phase of his analysis he had recognized through several clear dreams that if he could get the therapist to "throw him out" the patient would have considered this a victory in behalf of his moral masochism.

Since the therapist was on guard against this maneuver and had enough insight into his countertransference not to be challenged by this episode, the patient resorted to a much earlier form of omnipotent acting out: he again played "mother against father," since he knew that in his family mother controlled the money and paid all bills. It was indeed his mother who made contact with the therapist, wondering whether she should continue to pay for sessions that were missed since, according to her son, he had not been coming regularly lately. But aside from the waste of money, the mother wondered whether it was good for the son to feel guilty for causing his family expenses that were of no benefit to him.

Clearly, the patient was using the economic bind, the role-playing of earlier childhood, to maneuver therapy into a stalemate. Precisely because he was no longer a young adolescent, but a young adult who paid part of his expenses and lived by himself, the family could not use pressure or heavy authority, but had to leave decisions "up to him." It would go beyond the scope of this chapter to discuss the solution of this maneuver in detail; however it was resolved by the therapist remaining firm in his original position: to settle all therapeutic problems between himself and the patient.

The opposite situation occurred when a therapist made contact with the family when her patient began to miss sessions and acted out in other ways. In this case the referral triangle had been more overt from the start, inasmuch as the family who lived in a distant state from the therapist's office had made the first contact with the therapist and successfully put her in loco parentis. It was though the therapist had felt responsible to the family, rather than to the brilliant and difficult young undergraduate who was her patient. In addition, he came from a wealthy family who had used money to control him and his siblings, doling out the minimum necessary and insisting on exact accounting of all expenses. Of course, the family paid all therapeutic expenses, asking for monthly bills, bypassing the patient when it came to discussion of fees, manner of payment, and the entire financial aspect of the therapeutic contract.

By not safeguarding the transference but by acting out her countertransference, the therapist lost the patient who said he felt caught in a trap, since the family control which had dominated his entire life now reached into the office of the one person whom he had tried to trust.

Since there was considerable pathology, the young adult sought and found another therapist who considered the young man's identity crisis, his self-image dilemma, and the end of role-playing so tangled with the economic bind that he, after a few preliminary, exploratory sessions and a thorough psychologic diagnostic testing program, arrived at a bold, long-range program: he told the patient that he was very gifted, very mixed up and absolutely needed therapy—but independent of his family, which meant that the patient had to work full-time for a year or two, continue his studies on a part-time basis, and concentrate his energies on working out his problems. Since the young man had not been able to function academically in two of the nation's outstanding colleges, the therapist saw no harm in postponing the patient's academic education for a few years, during which he would experience both the desperately sought-for economic independence from his family's "chains"—as the patient put it—and work intensively on the resolution of his problems, preparing him to function eventually both in school and his profession.

Since the young man was not able to earn enough to pay for his own maintenance and for therapy, the analyst both lowered his fee and made a financial agreement with the patient which would allow him to owe a certain amount until he would be able to repay his debts. This was done on a definite, businesslike basis—comparable to a bank loan—to avoid accumulation of guilt, but based on the patient's personality as the only "security." It was this expression of trust in the sound ego-core of the young adult that formed the foundation of a successful therapeutic relationship. The referral triangle here was bypassed by a definite emphasis on "psychoanalytic treatment as a two-party contractual relationship."[44]

Where the self-image dilemma is particularly severe, the referral triangle poses particular challenges. The daughter of a divorced, successful businesswoman made contact with a therapist "at my mother's suggestion." It became clear in two exploratory interviews that this young college student was caught in her ambivalent strivings, unable to move in any direction without painful conflict against which she had built a defense of smiling indifference and blandness. In spite of the seemingly typical adolescent rebellious attitude toward mother and authority, the patient was existing in a deeply unconscious symbiotic relationship with her mother, whose control was covered with an attractive liberal and sophisticated veneer.

Because the control was extremely subtle and seemingly reasonable, the young woman had developed a strong, punitive superego—in conflict with one of her ego-ideals—which unsuccessfully demanded an equal place in her self-image. Her token rebellions consisted in small, inconsequential feuds with late-room monitors in high school, dormitory supervisors in college, stage managers in the drama lab where she was volunteering several evenings—over points of order, minor decisions, hairsplitting, obsessional details which gave her the illusion of independence. Realistically, because of her inability to invest libido in relationships or work, she was not functioning well in any area and accepted her mother's and college advisor's suggestion that she seek professional help.

The opening sentences of the psychologic report characterize the self-image dilemma:

"Although the patient seemed to want to comply with requirements of the situation, wanted to relate in a pleasant, cooperative manner, underlying negativism and hostility were only thinly veiled. Judging by her test responses, this young woman experiences uncertainty, conflict and at times near-confusion in practically all areas of functioning. No matter what takes place, she does not feel really in tune with what is going on around her or with what she thinks is expected of her, what she should feel or do . . ."

She felt that she should see a therapist and came with the same, pleasant, cooperative manner which the psychologist had noted in her test report, only to display the bland indifference on top of her negativism in every one of her exchanges with the therapist. When the therapist greeted her in the waiting room with a friendly "good evening," she did not respond except with an enigmatic smile. She made it clear in her particular indirect manner that she was here as a representative of mother and college advisor and would cooperate, no matter what.

She obediently listed her symptoms—with a few technical terms here and there—mentioned in passing "even a dream" she had had before coming: "something about walking out of the play in the first act" to which she had some associations which, however, she "did not want to talk about." When the therapist suggested that she was not too sure that she needed therapy, the young woman said with a smile that she was not sure about anything and why should she be sure about this? Besides, this was her mother's idea and who knows that it may do her some good? In the second, exploratory interview, the young woman reacted to the therapist with passivity, except to indicate that there had been things on her mind which she, however, did not want to talk about. She was willing to put in an appearance—to appease the superego or the incorporated mother image—but unwilling to say things out loud that she could not even admit to herself, in her own mind.

When, in addition, the young woman could not find free hours which coincided with the therapist's schedule and was unwilling to change dance class or weekend trips, the therapist suggested that the young woman might wait with therapy until later in her life, when she felt that this was necessary. He shared some of the psychologic findings, outlined the broad area of her ambivalence, and invited her to return when her schedule would coincide with his. He supported her ego-ideal by emphasizing the casually mentioned wish to have her own apartment, as a very understandable idea, and hoped that she would be able to carry out this plan before too long.

He further safeguarded the potential relationship by not sharing anything with the mother who called to inquire why her daughter was not in treatment, and by a tactful explanation of why an interview with the mother would not be wise.

When, a year later, a crisis developed in the young woman's relationship with her boy friend—which she in part blamed on the lack of privacy—the defense of indifference and blandness began to crumble enough to bring the self-image dilemma to a head. At this point, she wrote a note to the therapist, inquiring whether he "cared to see me" and began therapy.

She started her first session with the ego-ideal support from the exploratory interview twelve months earlier: the search for a home of her own.

It would seem as though in this situation, where the self-image dilemma had been particularly severe, the referral triangle posed a temporary impasse to therapy, as long as the superego representative—the energetic mother—determined the motivation for therapy. Both the expressed confidence in the patient's wishes to wait with treatment—though not openly verbalized—and the support of her wish for her own apartment represented a strengthening of the ego-ideal, which after an acute crisis in her life, tipped the balance of the dilemma enough for the patient to consider resolving the ambivalent strivings.

In this and the previous illustration of the referral triangle, the family of the patient represented one of the three sides. There are many, equally complex situations in which the referral of a young adult has not come from the family—directly or indirectly—but originated with a member of the community. In these instances too we need to be alert to the potential of a referral triangle with the ensuing complications for therapy. A few illustrations may clarify this further.

A young graduate student was referred by a neighbor, a high school teacher who had some previous professional contact with the therapist. It was not the patient himself who made the first contact but the teacher, who had come to know the patient through his relationships with her daughter.

The teacher had become concerned about the young man's anxiety, his loss of weight, and what she considered a paranoid trend, which she believed the young man may have "taken over from his mother" who had been in a state hospital for several years with a diagnosis of "paranoid schizophrenia." Since the young man was not only her daughter's boy friend but had also become somebody the teacher herself was very fond of, she was very concerned that he work out his problems. She had "taken the liberty of suggesting professional help for him" and had mentioned the therapist's name. The young man— she reported—had asked her to make the first contact.

The young therapist, who was not particularly concerned about the danger of a referral triangle, gave the woman an appointment for the patient and with this simple step set in motion the complications of a triangular relationship, with all the classical oedipal features. Because of a mistaken sense of professional courtesy—or perhaps because he needed the good will of a potential referral source for the future—the therapist failed to separate the referral source from the patient by not asking the young man to call himself for an appointment. He allowed the teacher to make the appointment and agreed to her suggestion to keep the fee as modest as possible because of the young man's strained circumstances.

When the young man arrived for his first session, he behaved exactly as an adolescent who had been sent by his mother, using the referral source to enforce his resistances: "Mrs. Frey suggested that I see you."

This familiar gambit can be avoided if we ask potential adolescent patients to call for their first appointment. It is certainly a requirement for young adults.

While this initial delay can be overcome in a relatively short time, the involvement of the referral party in the treatment process is more complicated.

For the first two years of his therapy, the patient used the teacher who had referred him to re-enact the childhood pattern of playing mother against father. When he could not accept the fee set by the therapist, when he could not accept an interpretation, when he repressed hostile feelings in the transference—he poured them out to his neighbor, the teacher-mother-referral party. The teacher, in turn, having been responsible for the therapeutic contact, took it upon herself to side with or against the patient, to attempt to influence the therapist by telephone or letters, and on two occasions asked for an appointment.

The therapist allowed this interference by continuing occasional contacts with the teacher, although her interference never came through associations by the patient. Indeed, the patient censored his contacts with the teacher, particularly remarks that were critical of the therapist. When once, after a particularly long pause, the therapist inquired into the silence, the patient blushed and explained that he had just run into the teacher on the street who wanted to know how much longer therapy would last. Since this had been the first comment about the referral source, the therapist encouraged his patient to tell him more about these inquiries and suggested that the patient may have mixed feelings about a neighbor wanting to know so much about his therapy. It was then that the patient expressed his first hostile feelings about the "nosy" neighbor to whom he probably should be very grateful but toward whom he felt also resentful. Since this young man had had real difficulties facing his homosexual conflicts, the long delay in associating freely had unnecessarily complicated the complex transference. Much of this could have been bypassed if the therapist had been aware of the many ways in which the referral triangle can lead to acting out of the oedipal situation in postadolescence.

While the problem in this situation had been the lack of separation between referral source and patient, the following case will suggest another aspect of the referral triangle: the history of the previous relationship between referral source and patient. The illustration is taken from the case of the young lesbian whose analysis has been discussed in Chapter 2.

We had mentioned that this young woman acted out her partially repressed wishes with substitutes and on one occasion chose for this purpose the original referral source at the time when the therapist did not rule for or against the planned separation from her husband. We had said: "She left her husband and moved into the apartment of the young woman who originally had suggested my name to her. She repeated the oedipal wish and regression by saying to me: If you will not support me and tell me what to do, you do not love me, so that I have no choice but to return to the woman who had sent me to you. If father does not love me the way I want him to, I have no choice but to return to mother."

The patient then lived with the woman who had referred her for two years and acted with her the way she had toward her mother, as described before.

It was only at this point of the analysis that I became fully aware of the significance of the referral source, the necessity to understand the history and the latent transference which exists between referral source and patient in postadolescence and after.

While the nature of the transference in a trusted friend, somebody whose advice one seeks, has been fully described, there remains a particular aspect of this constellation which seems to me to be a function of the postadolescent characteristics. In childhood and adolescence, advice is frequently taken because of (or in spite of) superego representatives; in adult life, the choice of advisors has a more voluntary character, since we are assuming the existence of a more autonomous ego function. In postadolescence, where the depersonalization aspects of the identity struggle inundate the ego autonomy, where psychosexual confusion is rampant (as in the case of this young woman), we can expect less objectivity in the choice of advisors, particularly when the self-image vascillates sharply between ego-ideal and superego, and the young adult shifts his confidence accordingly from one trusted to a formerly suspect object. Some young adults go to some lengths in collecting information about a potential source of authority, as insurance against their own understandable doubts about their own autonomous judgment. It seems to be reasonable to suggest that young adults, more than people in their later years, tend to invest and withdraw libido in authority figures, particularly when they have to make decisions which are in conflict with family or community. The choice of the advisor—among many potential ones—is particular and significant for the understanding of the initial transference in therapy. It is likely that the person whose advice the young adult seeks represents one or the other aspect of his self-image dilemma: a superego or an ego-ideal representative. Once the advisor has made his suggestion, the post-adolescent is likely to expect to use the therapist in the same way in which he had chosen the referral source. As one patient put it when asked about his reasons for the choice of a therapist: "If Bob recommends him, I know the doctor must be right for me, he would be a Bob-kind of person, straightforward, smart and with a sense of humor."

This extension of the original transference from the referral source to the therapist is of interest in the handling of the first phase of analysis, as well as the most meaningful management of the transference.

I had not sufficiently considered the nature of the relationship between the referral source and the previous patient, nor considered their history. The young woman who had sent the patient to me had seen me once for a consultation, many years ago, at the request of her boy friend, my patient. Their affair had been gradually dissolving, and I had seen her to find a therapist for her. Since the purpose of the consultation was strictly limited I did not want to probe but remembered having considered the possibility of her homosexuality. I did not know what became of her, since the young man, who had been my patient, separated from her and spoke little of her. Apparently she had had a brief marriage, which also dissolved. However, she used the married name which my patient mentioned when she first contacted me. If I had been more aware of the referral triangle and the implications for the transference, I should have inquired more into the background of the referring party, without disturbing the patient. I remember having asked who had sent her to me and was told an unknown name of a "friend" who recommended me highly because I had once helped a friend of hers. Apparently my narcissism prevented me from inquiring into the history of this "friend" or I could have learned a great deal about the relationship between patient and the referral source. I might have been able to glean some knowledge of her self-image dilemma from the choice of a friend who—as I learned two years later—turned out to be another homosexual object choice, which was used for acting-out purposes in the transference. Only when the patient moved in with the other woman—at the point when I "disappointed" her—did I realize that throughout the analysis the patient had frequently consulted this woman and expressed hostile feelings about the analysis which she had censored in the sessions. With more awareness on my part of the significance of the referral source, I could have inquired into the history of this relationship and possibly anticipated some of the subsequent developments.

This would have been particularly significant in this last illustration because of the patient's tendency to act out partially repressed wishes with substitutes, as well as her difficulty of giving up the end of role-playing (the mother-child game in the basic homosexual constellation).

It would be equally significant in all cases where the self-image crisis is pronounced, with the unavoidable tendency to vascillate sharply between ego-ideals and superego representatives.

Where certain aspects of the identity diffusion have produced some of the postadolescent symptoms, we frequently find the young adult seeking relief from such painful experiences as depersonalization or estrangement by confiding in a friend or a trusted member of the community. This relationship often functions as a substitute for therapy and is used in behalf of the resistances until the point is reached where professional help becomes unavoidable. It follows that the resistance now takes another path: an attempt to cling to the trusted friend in spite of the intellectual recognition that a trained, objective source is more helpful. In this struggle the patient will use the friend and the therapist to act out some of the basic oedipal conflicts via the referral triangle.

If this constellation can be recognized at the outset, complications can be avoided during the clinical work.

9. The Initial Consultation

IN ORDER TO CREATE from the beginning a climate in which the watch-fulness of the superego can be relaxed, we would want to avoid comments or attitudes that suggest watchfulness on our part, i.e., we do not want to create the impression that the postadolescent patient is being watched or judged in any way. In practical terms we would avoid "shrewd or insightful" observations or any suggestions that sound like special insights or awareness of his problems that he himself has not already expressed.

After the therapeutic process has been under way for a time, during which we attempt to modify the severities of their rigid superego structures, our young adult patients will use us most likely as their superego to avoid increase of guilt or a protection against acting out. However, this development cannot start in the beginning and in no case during the consultation, where this climate may easily lead to negative transference, unnecessarily complicating the work ahead.

As it is, we will have to demand a certain fee, announce certain hours which may complicate the patients' lives, introduce some basic rules—in short, we are, *nolens volens*, in a somewhat authoritarian position, in addition to the awe in which many young people hold workers in our profession. When Glover cautions against "too spurious a professional attitude" and states that "the besetting sins of psycho-analytical practice are smugness, timidity, hyper-sensitivity and ritualism,"[45] we would suggest that this is particularly valid for the young adult who, because of his position, is himself hypersensitive to any behavior that smacks of parental authority.

On the other side, young adults have complained about the false joviality and condescending neutrality which they had encountered in initial consultations. In order not to structure the transference, some therapists begin their passive listening as soon as possible after the young adult has entered the office, creating unnecessary tension and anxiety in the patient who can not know what is expected of him.

We do structure the transference, whether we are active or passive, and for this reason it would seem advisable to be definite in the image we are creating from the start. The more we succeed in remaining on the level the patient has reached, the more the patient can accept our demands. For a simple illustration, take the matter of how to address the patient on first sight in the waiting room. (For a fuller discussion on the significance of names in the organization of ego defenses, see Murphy.[46]) It seems natural and realistic to address the patient by the name which he himself has used in his first telephone contact with us: "You are Bob Jones, I am Dr. Smith." This would be different from introducing ourselves to a younger adolescent who has been referred as "Bob" and would feel alienated if we did not say, "Hi, Bob." Young adults are sensitive about being addressed by their first name by a stranger but would feel awkward if we used the conventional "Mr." If the referral has been made by a third party, it is helpful to ask what the young adult patient calls himself.

If we are not sure how to address the patient, we might ask him and get a first glimpse at the self-image dilemma. A young graduate student explained that his name was "Robert Hartley the Second, after my father and grandfather. My parents call me Bob, but I prefer just plain 'Chuck'."

When interest was expressed in the origin of this nickname, he said that this was his fraternity name, and began to talk about the significance of his reference group, his girl friend, and led into his conflict over his self-image dilemma.

We had in fact begun our diagnostic interview, which needs some modifications because of the particular postadolescent characteristics.

Since several authors have suggested systematic outlines for the psychoanalytic diagnostic interview, there is no need here to repeat the essential content that should be covered in the initial consultation. Instead, we might consider how the usual requirements could be adapted to the postadolescent characteristics.

I am taking as a point of departure Leon Saul's paper,[47] in which he suggests that "a bird's-eye view, a clear perspective of the causal forces should be gained in the very first interview. It is usually exceedingly difficult to obtain once treatment is under way, and may not emerge sharply until after the end of the analysis."

Because we are behaving differently in this initial consultation than during the rest of the therapeutic experience characterized by free association, I have found it helpful to tell the new patient that this is a consultation in which I hope to get an overview of his personality, so that I will have to ask many questions and would like to take notes, with his permission.

Saul suggests that we get (a) anamnestic data, (b) conscious attitudes, and (c) unconscious associative material.

On top of the anamnestic data he lists: "chief complaints, current life and emotional involvements."

We might add "sociopsychologic characteristics of the postadolescent, when interviewing the current life situation." If, for example, the economic bind presents a highly charged issue for the young adult, an issue which possibly overlaps with the self-image dilemma, this may affect our decision as to the preferred form of therapy. I am thinking, for an illustration, of a young man to whom economic independence from his family was of such paramount importance—at the time of his consultation—that he was absolutely unwilling to accept any financial help for a four-times-a-week analysis, for which he psychologically would have been ready. He earned enough money to pay for two sessions, and while he intellectually understood the advantages of a full analysis, he felt strongly that the resentment against having to accept help from his family would have outweighed any gain which the full analysis might have made. Although he changed this position during the first year of his therapy, for the time being it seemed necessary to respect his wishes —with an understanding of the implications of the economic bind—and plan a more limited, two-times-a-week form of analytic psychotherapy.

The second item suggested under anamnestic data is: "habits, routine, a typical day." Again we might add for our postadolescent patients, cognition of time continuity, since most young adults express some of their disorganization in the management of time during a typical day. Particularly where young adults live by themselves, I would pay attention to the degree to which they have been able to establish a realistic time routine (going to bed and getting up at definite hours, management of appointments, classes, or long-term assignments).

For the third item, "onset and course of complaints and symptoms," it would seem particularly helpful to concentrate with the postadolescent patient on the time immediately prior to his coming to the initial consultation, since he most likely will be more willing to share this information than the history, even as far as his conscious recollection is concerned. This too, like the previous item, is due to the time-continuity characteristic. In addition, a detailed description of the state of the ego during the moment of decision to call a therapist for an appointment usually gives us a direct, first-hand and nonintellectual view.

The fourth item, "significant interrelationships at various ages in childhood," should probably be modified to read, current reference group and history of friendship circles, as far back as patient can trace it, because of the particular significance the peer group has in post-adolescence.

The fifth point, "medical history, including symptoms, psychologic and physical," needs emphasis for young adults who usually are not concerned with their medical history because of their age and frequently tend to ignore even persistent symptoms in the present. One young man who mentioned headaches which he called psychosomatic actually suffered from astigmatism for a period of time, as diagnosed by the ophthalmologist. On the other side, one young woman who suffered from chest pains at infrequent intervals was certain that she had a "heart murmur," which she used as a defense for her passive fantasies. On examination, no organic basis for the chest pains was found and indeed this symptom never occurred again after analysis had been under way for some time.

The second topical heading, *"conscious attitudes,"* begins with attitudes "toward others, especially during the earliest years and present." One might consider here in particular the postadolescent characteristics as discussed in "Group Formation and Isolation," in order to establish whether, for example, the isolate position evolved during adolescence and after, or whether this had been a more basic role in early childhood. I have found a consistent pattern of a history of early isolation from nursery school on in borderline or schizophrenic patients, while the character disorders functioned well in early groups until puberty, when the process of isolation began to become obvious.

The second item under "conscious attitudes" is "patient's attitudes toward an understanding of himself, his symptoms, and his problems." This is the place where we would want to pay particular attention to aspects of the identity struggle, depersonalization aspects, and psychosexual diffusion, as discussed in the first chapter.

This would give us both material for our understanding of the patient and judgment about his ability to tolerate the development of a transference neurosis and uncovering of defenses. If the depersonalization aspects—as part of the postadolescent identity struggle—are too prominent during the initial consultation, we would want to think of a more limited form of analytic therapy, with the possibility of moving into a full analytic experience later on.

The third item, called "views of his future, his expectations and ambitions," should be considered with particular emphasis on the self-image dilemma in postadolescence, which would be visible when we talk with our prospective patient about his professional or vocational plans.

We would want to differentiate between the ego-ideal and the pseudoideal, representing infantile, omnipotent strivings; the determinants of the superego aspects in the self-image and the degree of conflict between them.

The outline suggests as the next item, "conventional examination of mental status," which had better be eliminated with young adults, particularly if they are in college or graduate school, where their mental status is frequently tested and evaluated. The fifth item, "major forces in the personality," begins with "psychosexual," which would be the place to try to understand some of the psychosexual aspects of the identity diffusion, which are usually present in post-adolescence. In spite of their overt sexual behavior at this time, we do look for masculine-feminine diffusion, compensatory and defensive aspects of the sexual identity. The degree of role-playing, for example, in sexual acting out should be ascertained in the initial consultation for an evaluation of the integration of ego forces.

"Dependence and independence," the next heading under "major forces in the personality," should be understood against all the characteristics of this particular phase of growth, i.e., we want to try to evaluate how much dependence or independence we can expect, given sufficient knowledge of the identity diffusion, the self-image dilemma, and the relatively fluctuating state of the ego forces. The same goes for "needs for love and object interests," particularly if we have determined the limitations of the previously mentioned factors.

Saul suggests that we attempt to assess "feelings of inferiority, egotism, narcissism, competitiveness toward members of family . . ." which seems to be written in particular for the postadolescent, although the outline is meant for all patients, regardless of age. We should add in our young adult patients a differential note on "narcissism": Because of the particular state of the ego at this phase of growth, we may want to evaluate degrees of healthy and pathologic narcissism, as discussed earlier in the book.

Another issue which frequently is of concern to workers with post-adolescent patients is the use of projective tests. It is by now generally accepted that if tests are to be given, they should be administered by somebody other than the therapist who plans to treat the patient, because the role of tester unnecessarily complicates the transference. This general practice should be particularly stressed for the post-adolescent patient who often still considers all tests measures of achievements and tends to think of "passing" or "failing," in spite of his intellectual knowledge about the meaning of projective tests. We suggested earlier that we would want to avoid in the initial consultation any comment or attitude that would suggest to the patient that he is being judged in any way. Since taking tests sometimes has this meaning for young adults, we had better refer the patient to an experienced clinical psychologist for testing, if we consider tests necessary.

This determination depends on the particular case and the judgment of the clinician, however. A few general comments can be made about young peoples' reactions to tests. Aside from the temporary anxiety about "passing" or "failing," most postadolescents have had definite reactions to the taking of tests, which were of diagnostic significance. A number of young adults would express hesitation or outright refusal to tests, which turned out to be a form of resistance of "being seen." The way they put it was: "I don't want anybody else to know more about me than I do," suggesting rivalry with the therapist and competition with the "authority," first glimpses at the oedipal constellation.

For many postadolescents, the idea of taking tests was "fun," suggesting narcissistic gratifications and possibly an anticipation of strengthening their intellectual defenses: after the tests I will "know" more about myself.

This raises the final question in the initial interview: how to use test reports in a second consultation. The alert, intelligent young adult who has some general knowledge of psychologic tests would like to know some of the content of the summary report. We will be creating unnecessary antagonisms by withdrawing to a "professional" position and announcing that these reports are confidential and not meant for the patient.

In fact, a carefully selected reading of some of the outstanding diagnostic findings in the psychologic report can be of help to the patient in getting a first objective statement about his pathology. It will be related to the symptoms that had brought him to the consultation, but it will put them in the framework of his total personality and history. Where I have had occasion to use tests and have shared some of the findings in the initial consultation—always related to the material that he had given me in the beginning—patients have frequently remembered these statements and come back to them, sometimes a year or two later, when the clinical material through their associations confirmed the original diagnosis.

10. "Variations" in Technique

ALTHOUGH THERE IS evidence for assuming that only a small percentage of postadolescents can be fully analyzed, it is not necessary to abandon the basis of the classical technique within the analytic psychotherapy which is possible for young adult patients. It is rather like traveling a solid, tried road which will have occasional detours but then lead back to the main highway. The "detours" will be the educational aspects of analytic therapy necessary for postadolescents. Because of the particular clinical problems the young adult presents, some colleagues have not only taken the detours but stayed on it too long, never finding their way back to the mainstream of classical procedure. They have gone from variations in technique to modifications, from exploratory therapy to educational suggestion.

The 20th Congress of the International Psychoanalytical Association in Paris in 1957, dealt extensively with the topic, "Variations in Classical Psycho-Analytical Technique."[48] In his "Remarks on Some Variations," Rudolph Lowenstein, in a footnote, distinguished between the two concepts:

> As *modifications,* in contradistinction to *variations,* I would mainly describe changes in three areas of the analytic process: (I) Any tendency to curtail the spontaneous production of the patient, with the resultant neglect of understanding his unconscious. (II) Minimization of the interpretative work in favor of manipulative interventions; i.e., procedures that diminish reliance on insight achieved in the patient by verbalization and working through, in favor, e.g., of transference results or "corrective emotional experiences," etc. (III) Such modifications of the optimal conditions for an analysis as hamper the patient's analysibility; e.g. those jeopardizing the formation or resolution of the transference neurosis.

Lowenstein is here referring to educational psychotherapy, which Freud anticipated in a mass application of psychoanalysis, when he spoke of "alloying the pure gold of analysis freely with the copper of direct suggestion."[49] This is not a variation of the exploratory therapy which identifies the classical technique, but a modification which Glover discussed in more detail in his *Technique of Psychoanalysis,* where he characterizes such techniques as "pseudo-analytical suggestions."[45]

"There is one feature in common to all these methods," Glover says, "they are all backed by strong transference authority, which means that by sharing the guilt with the suggestionist and by borrowing strength from the suggestionist's superego, a new substitution product is accepted by the patient's ego. The new 'therapeutic symptom construction' has become, for the time, ego-syntonic."

From our previous discussion of the postadolescent's self-image dilemma, these modifications of classical technique would not be applicable to the young adult who often is in the midst of a severe conflict between his ego-ideal and his superego. He will be prevented from resolving this dilemma if the "suggestionist" permits him to borrow strength from his superego, which will tip the balance in favor of the patient's superego, instead of weighing it against the ego-ideal and resolving it through an exploratory process; that is, reducing it to the basic elements, or in brief, analyzing it.

Put in the simplest terms possible, the modifications of classical technique, the reliance on education and suggestion, is not useful for most of our postadolescent patients, because it does not stand up for more than a very brief period; it does not work.

At the same time, we are aware of the fact that the classical technique is not usually possible for the postadolescent. What then are variations of classical technique which are effective with the young adult patient?

The problem of variations—like variations on a theme in music—have long been familiar to analysts of children and adolescents. The literature of child analysis is replete with theoretic and practical discussions of this theme, perhaps beginning with Anna Freud's *Introduction to Techniques of Child Analysis,* in 1929,[41] followed by the successive annual volumes of the "Psychoanalytic Study of the Child," from 1945 ·to the present.

The particular variations for the treatment of adolescents have been described in these volumes, as well as in the previously mentioned panel discussion where K. R. Eissler differentiated between characteristic adolescent symptoms—requiring special techniques—and the "bona fide neurosis" that we encounter in adults. He suggests:

> The psychopathology encountered in adolescent patients may manifest itself into two main forms. It may be solidified, unchanging, well-established, that is to say, structured like the equivalent syndrome in the adult. Thus an adolescent may need treatment because of a full-fledged compulsive-obsessional neurosis; or he may have a long history of delinquency that has now become so intensified that he is in open conflict with society; or he may be fixated on an outspoken sexual aberration.
> The other form of psychopathology is not solidified but still in flux. Then symptoms of quite different syndromes may coexist or appear inter-

mittently. The final channel for the discharge of conflict has not yet been decided.

In the first-mentioned instance . . . no technical difficulties are encountered that differ essentially from those . . . in the adult. The adolescent suffering from a bona fide compulsion neurosis will be treated like his adult counterpart (with certain qualifications). The adolescent who is still groping in search of a style, however, sets technical problems,[50] that, in their magnitude, are not encountered in other clinical situations.

These same considerations apply to some postadolescent patients, in particular for our diagnostic understanding as it evolves through the gradual unfolding of the material and affects our techniques of therapy.

As in adolescence, the hard-core pathology has to be differentiated from some of the postadolescent characteristics: A young adult may appear in the opening stage to be suffering from a severe hysteria-anxiety, bordering on schizoid states, while we really are observing depersonalization aspects of the identity diffusion that we had discussed in the opening chapter. Some acting-out young adults may appear to have impulse disorders, while their behavior should perhaps be seen as part of the postadolescent's difficulty to come to terms with the end of role-playing, as described before. What may appear as a genuine character disorder should perhaps be understood as the manifestation of a serious self-image dilemma.

Most often we will find both solidified pathology and the still fluctuating, but transitory symptoms of postadolescence, so that in practice we can not rely on any one technique in postadolescence but need to vary them in accordance with the clinical necessities. As Eissler suggests in the previously quoted paper: "The analyst must have at his command techniques with which to deal with neuroses, perversions, schizophrenia and delinquency."

What are the variations, the variety of flexible techniques that the analyst might use in analytic psychotherapy with postadolescents?

In spite of the mature veneer of many postadolescent patients and their often outstanding intellectual maturity, the young adult seems to require some of the same active, outgoing attitude on our part that we have come to develop with adolescents. If we use the concept of compassionate neutrality as a basic analytic attitude with all our patients, the accent might well be on "compassionate" when it comes to young adults, who have come for resolution of basic conflicts and feel particularly ambivalent toward the process from the start, in part as a result of the self-image dilemma.

In addition to the expected resistance—the basic omnipotent position —which we will have to work with throughout the analytic process, there is another form of realistic interference which is in large measure due to the characteristics of the postadolescent situation. Many young adults who have come to the conclusion that they need professional help have usually read a good deal, taken courses in various aspects of psychology, and discussed forms of psychotherapy or schools of analytic thought. This intellectual interest often leaves them quite troubled and confused, doubtful over what they should expect and suspicious of what they hear from teachers, older friends, or the therapist they came to see.

It is a truism to state that this intellectual hesitation and doubt will be used in the service of the unconscious resistances; however, we cannot help but deal first with the surface interferences if we hope to get a chance to reach the basic ones. Contrary to the maneuvers of the adolescent patient and quite different from the manifest rationalizations of adult patients, early resistances of the postadolescent patient cannot be countered by a withdrawal to a passive position, which will be experienced as an evasion of their questions. If the young adult asks about analytic orientation, our theoretic position, or schools of training, we would gain in the long run if we attempted to answer their often misplaced and confusing questions as directly and simply as we are able to. While it is axiomatic, as Glover suggests, that "nothing is more obstructive to analytic progress than to commence work by taking sides on controversial issues,"[43] we also cannot afford to evade their rationalizations by withdrawal to humorless or stodgy pronouncements about our professional role.

These questions sometimes come up in connection with the patient's concern over the use of the couch. Since analysis is considered the "real thing" and since the cliche associates the process with the use of the couch, many young adults have questions about it.

Inasmuch as we are here considering not a complete, classical analysis but a more limited analytic therapy, the question arises whether the use of the couch is altogether appropriate. In spite of the many different practices currently in vogue, there is probably agreement that the couch should not be used with severely regressed or some borderline patients, who cannot make the transition from free association to reality, from primary to secondary process thinking without impairing their daily functioning. Sometimes younger therapists have suggested the use of the couch without being fully aware of the main function of this position: to encourage the development of a transference neurosis, as part of the classical analysis. While the use of the couch for other purposes may or may not be harmful to the therapeutic process, it would certainly not be helpful to ask a postadolescent patient to use the couch in order to encourage his illusion that he is "under analysis"— getting the most intensive therapy possible. As a general practice with young adults, sitting up on a twice-a-week basis has been satisfactory. There are exceptions of course, particularly when it has become obvious that the associations are severely restricted by sitting up and facing the therapist. However, we might be wary about young adults asking about the couch in the beginning and first explore what this request represents.

Aside from the possible use of the couch as an acting out of resistances, the sitting up in twice-a-week analytic therapy may be considered a safeguard, particularly with postadolescents where the differentiation between age-specific characteristics and genuine borderline states is not easy to make, at least in the opening phase of treatment.

Finally, in terms of the previously discussed differences between variation and modification, the exploratory versus the educational form of therapy, the couch would tend to encourage regression and by the same token transference authority, which would be counter to any form of analytic, exploratory therapy.

At the same time, just because we are trying to create an informal atmosphere, we want to be sure to watch for the many familiar forms of resistances. Among these are such things as starting the session in the waiting room, bringing up important material or dreams at the end of the hour or on the way out, in other words, avoiding the structure of the analytic relationship by turning it into a social discussion session, frequent phone calls or cancellations, frequent changes of the appointment, bringing a friend to the waiting rom while the session is in progress, avoiding discussion of payments, patterns of not paying the monthly bill or forgetting to pay, delaying the session by making out the check in the office, receiving phone calls in the analyst's office, to mention some of the characteristic resistances, particularly in the beginning of the therapeutic relationship. It has often been helpful, particularly with young adults in college, to state the groundrules in the beginning of the relationship. Many postadolescent patients have been conditioned to expect some statement of procedures and rules. One young adult put it well when he said to his therapist, after having accepted the need for treatment: "How do we go about it?"

Particularly with the bright and sophisticated young adult, it is helpful to be very candid about the whole of the therapeutic process: the difficulties in learning to free-associate, the probable length of therapy, the possible results one can reasonably expect. Intelligent young people are offended when they are told to just go ahead and say whatever comes to mind, as though this were an easy task; they feel talked down to when somebody tells them that the length of treatment "depends"; they feel rightfully treated as children when they hear about the results of therapy, that one has to wait and see. They feel that these statements are not sincere, but evasive generalizations, designed to establish the oracle-like wisdom of the therapist. They are never experienced as an expression of modesty or lack of knowledge on our part, though this may well be the reason for our responses.

The bright young adult who has relied on his intellect to cope with his ego deficiencies will need considerable encouragement to allow himself to express thoughts and feelings that "make no sense" at the moment, that seem illogical or irrational. It may be helpful to anticipate this difficulty and let him know that everything within him and his previous training will object to letting out "meaningless" or "ridiculous" sentences or ideas. We might be more helpful and realistic to point out in the beginning that it will take time to learn this new way of speaking.

Where young people have been realistically concerned with the usual length of the therapeutic experience, I have found it sometimes helpful to refer to such statistics as the length of training of analytic students in the major training institutes in the United States, as reported by Lewin and Ross,[51] where eight hundred hours were found to be an average, for a full analysis, with allowance for variations. Since we frequently do not plan a full analysis, it seems realistic to refer to this figure as a general guideline and emphasize that while in the work planned less time will be required, it will take a few hundred hours in any case to produce any significant changes. The young adult, used to thinking in terms of years of college or graduate school, does not usually realize that two hours weekly therapy add up to about a hundred hours a year, with vacations. It is realistic to ask them to plan for staying two or three years at least, if the work and money invested is to be worth the effort. That this means planning their study or work, their residence and budget is understood.

Contrary to some colleagues, I cannot find the young adult's question about the results of analytic therapy unjustified. They have a right to ask what they can expect for the work and money invested, just as with any other service rendered in our society. Indeed, if one cannot anticipate the modification of some very troublesome symptoms, the reduction of pain that interferes with the pleasure of living, the resolution of some of the major interferences, a clarification of the self-image dilemma, a more realistic approach to the problems of everyday life— one might do better to refer the prospective patient to somebody else. Certainly we have no written guarantees, but we can make reasonable assumptions, based on our professional experience and confidence. We anticipate hard work on the part of ourselves and our patient, but unless we can have a positive expectation for the outcome, it will be very difficult for the patient to sustain the many dark moments in the therapeutic process.

11. Variations, II: Transference and Countertransference

WE ARE PROCEEDING with the assumption that in many, if not most, postadolescent cases, we will be able to work with the patient on a twice-weekly basis, usually sitting up, which determines our structuring of the transference. It also presents some particular problems of countertransference, especially when we are confronted with a severe self-image dilemma.

Since we, in this assumption, are not aiming at a complete analysis, we are not attempting to develop a transference neurosis, but we make use of the transference in the more active technique which usually is required in analytic therapies. This raises some questions of technique in regard to the management of the transference, the style of free associations, and in particular, the handling of silence on both the part of the young adult patient and the analyst.

Because of the particular postadolescent characteristics, we will often encounter transference situations which are unexpected and markedly different from those seen in an adult neurosis. For an example we might consider a twenty-year-old college student with an intense sense of competition and feelings of deprivation who had been unable to perceive relationships during adolescence but after two years of therapy was able to have his first meaningful relationship with a girl. While his intense hostility, which was partially turned back on himself, had made for some degree of paranoid thinking, he was able to overcome some of his feeling of danger in the outside world and to control some of his impulsive acting out of hostile projections. His work in college as well as his relationship to his girl friend were satisfying—results based on what seemed to be a positive transference.

During the third year of therapy, the analyst received a phone call from the young man's mother who was concerned about her son's arrest by the police for driving without a license and peddling drugs. In reporting this, the mother mentioned that this was the second brush with the law, following his theft of books in the college bookstore. None of this had been shared with the therapist. While the patient had always freely verbalized his hostility toward "society," restricting laws, "middle-class morality," and said that he saw nothing wrong with breaking laws as long as one could get away with it, he had not reported that he had failed in acting out what could be called one of his ego-ideals or his pseudo-ego-ideal. In his dress and manner he had openly affiliated himself with what was called "the beatniks" in his community, although unlike many of his drug-addict friends, the patient had kept up with his school work and maintained a serious relationship with a girl from school, who also was a serious student.

It would seem that this patient had solved his self-image dilemma by projecting the superego aspect on his therapist, while he maintained the defective ego-ideal by identification with his overindulging mother. The transference in this case seems to have been based on a sharply split self-image, which could have been handled more effectively by more awareness of the countertransference on the therapist's part.

It would appear as though too many interpretations in this case had coincided with the patient's sugerego, which facilitated this self-image split and projection in the transference. An illustration of the ways in which the countertransference interfered may clarify this further.

Racker suggests that[52] "every transference situation provokes a countertransference situation, which arises out of the analyst's identification of himself with the (patient's) internal objects . . . every positive transference situation is answered by a positive countertransference; to every negative transference there responds, in one part of the analyst, a negative countertransference."

Although some clinicians would question this generalized formulation of countertransference, it remains of importance that the analyst remain aware of the potential danger of denying his latent reactions, particularly when they become apparent in his dreams.

It is the negative transference which interests us in this case where the young man's censure of his acting-out behavior represents a defense against his own accusing superego, which was projected on the analyst. The patient avoids the expected critical response, which in his case would be used in behalf of his paranoid thinking, a tendency which he has become aware of during his therapy. He presents the ego-ideal part of his self-image, but refers to the "bad" part of his ego indirectly, through veiled aggression against the analyst. He tells him that there is no use talking about the beatnik culture and philosophy, the need for detachment and remaining cool, avoiding involvement and all that to anybody over thirty years old. From his previous material it is clear that he is referring to his "square" father, but in the context of the session the analyst applies this statement to himself, since he, too, is clearly older than thirty years. Both the hostile statement about the lack of understanding of people of a certain age and the analyst's sensitivity about his age lead him to react to this negative transference with a negative countertransference. The analyst is really irritated by the patient's association, checks his anger and, instead of recognizing his negative countertransference, expresses it with counteraggression: he asks the young man what makes him think that he, the analyst, is incapable of understanding the beatnik culture. In other words, the analyst changes his understanding of the transference into a deficient interpretation by the unrecognized countertransference. He is in fact asking the patient not to resist, to trust him and to accept him as somebody different from his father. The patient's unconscious perceives this clearly, as expressed by a grin and an assurance that he was not referring to the analyst at all, but to people like his father or teachers. This is of course a denial of the internal reality of the patient, a reinforcement of his defenses, with surface compliance or "overcoming of the resistance." It is not too difficult to understand how a continuous lack of countertransference recognition would lead this patient to overdetermine the pseudo-ego-ideal and to censor the negative transference to the point where such material as driving without a license, or smoking marihuana, or taking drugs no longer came up in the session.

So far the illustration could have applied to an adult patient as well. What makes this different is the fact that the young adult used his mother to facilitate the censuring of the negative transference and, in the long run, to avoid resolving his self-image dilemma. Because of the economic bind, the socio-psychologic pressures that we had discussed in a general way before, we can understand that in this case the mother—who controlled the money in the home—could be used as a "confidante" for acting-out purposes. This particular mother, an intelligent, well-educated woman who had some definite ideas on the lack of freedom of young people, encouraged him to get his own apartment, for which she paid, standing by in every situation with one condition: that he be frank with her and never be afraid to discuss anything. In other words, by using mother and analyst as he had used mother and father—to play against one another, in early childhood and latency—the patient was able to continue acting out his infantile fantasies, encouraged by the analyst's unrecognized countertransference. Once the mother had made contact with the analyst and shared the censored material, the patient re-emphasized the pseudo-ego-ideal by assuring the analyst that this "delinquent" behavior had been one of his silly mistakes, which he deeply regretted. He emphasized his honor work in his major in college, his good relationship to his girl friend, his job—to prove that he was rapidly getting well and no longer needed to be in treatment. In spite of his analyst's warnings, the young man made it clear that he did not see any urgent need to be in treatment and after a few more months, discontinued therapy.

The combination of the sharply split self-image dilemma and the role of the mother in the typical postadolescent economic bind made for a transference and countertransference situation, which may be considered specific for the young adult patient.

While all countertransference reactions—such as annoyance, anxiety, overidentification, etc.—will occur with the young adult patient, as with other patients of any age, the countertransference aggression seems to be of particular interest with the postadolescent patient.

This may be due to the ways in which the postadolescent characteristics are expressed in the analytic transference, whether they are metapsychologic or sociopsychologic in origin. A typical example is the young adult in therapy whose father pays for the sessions, while the patient—for a number of complex reasons—frequently misses appointments. The analyst sees the missed sessions as a transference manifestation: the patient wants to hurt his father by wasting father's money, and he unconsciously rejects the analyst by wasting the time allotted to him. The analyst makes an interpretation directed against the acting out of the hostile wishes—the competition, the oedipal situation. The patient responds by laughter, frustrating the analyst. At this point the analyst identifies himself with the patient's father, the internalized object, by referring to the patient's behavior as "unfair." The patient perceives this countertransference by asking whose side the analyst is on, father or son.

"Countertransference reactions of aggression (or of its equivalent) occur in response to transference situations in which the patient frustrates certain desires of the analyst," as Racker points out.

The patient is succeeding in his attempt to bypass the interpretation, by the countertransference reaction of the analyst. As the young man said, many months later, when this material came up once more, as a result of a dream: "I put you down, when I asked you what side you are on." Apparently, the frustration which the analyst experienced led him to defend himself against the patient's attack by the same identification with the aggressor as the patient used. In fact, the analyst becomes "the persecutor."

The countertransference identification, which is always a hazard in child and adolescent analysis, still presents a source of danger to analytic exploration in postadolescence. It is not unusual to find oneself identifying with the young adult in his rejection of his family's values and to accept the role of the ego-ideal representative, which is particularly gratifying if the young adult has had several unsuccessful therapeutic experiences. The temptation to step out of the transference and use the authority invested in us is particularly strong when young people find themselves in situations which are clearly dangerous.

For an example we may consider the young woman who has lived in a hostile dependency relationship with her divorced mother, playing the role of the father in a latent homosexual seduction, together with a moral masochistic position, which Berliner characterized as "hanging on to a breast that is not there."[53] Like many character disorders that fall into this group, this young woman too needed to be "right rather than happy," a situation which made for a very complex transference situation from the very beginning.

In this patient where one could see the neurotic solution of the infantile conflict between the need for being loved and the actual experience of nonlove (in the widest sense) coming from the person whose love is needed, the transference was always characterized by the patient's need to accuse and complain, to be the troublemaker and the "victim." Berliner suggested in this same paper that we give "the analysis of the victim priority over the analysis of the troublemaker," and "slow down the development of an intense emotional transference to the person of the analyst."

The goal in the first phase of treatment is to help the patient to discover that she is consistently accusing love objects of mistreating her, that in some ways she had, without knowing it, chosen certain people to play certain roles in order to repeat her original relationship with her first love object, mother. Because this is a young adult who has not yet come to terms with the "end of role-playing" (as I termed one of the postadolescent characteristics), she would act out her role of troublemaker and victim in many situations, including the transference.

When the patient had succeeded in separating herself physically from her mother, moved into her own home and formed a first sexual relationship, the end of role-playing characteristics presented a particular challenge to the countertransference. Without being direct or facing the issue of pregnancy, the patient would suggest that she was playing first the troublemaker and then the victim by not taking proper precautions against impregnation. This, then, was clearly a situation where the analyst was tempted to rely on transference authority, acting out the countertransference of role-playing: the protective, cautioning parent, to become the better mother in the analytic situation.

The session in which this material came to a head also contained a very characteristic memory of this patient, following a dream. One of the associations was of herself in second grade, where the student-teacher had asked the children to draw a picture of their family. Because the teacher planned to use these drawings for a research project and wanted anonymity, she had asked the children not to write their names on the pictures. The patient not only did write her name, but upon handing it in, asked the teacher to repeat her request. When she was assured that she had done the wrong thing, she told the teacher about it in a defiant way and waited for her punishment. She remembered being somewhat disappointed that the teacher only smiled and scolded a little, after erasing the name.

She repeated this provocative troublemaker-victim role in the session when she announced that she did not like to use birth-control devices, because they were interfering with her pleasure. When the analyst remained silent, she went on to ask whether this was not dangerous and could lead to pregnancy. There still was no response to her provocation, upon which the young woman suggested that if she would have a baby she would just have to face it, although this would mean the interruption of her career as a dancer, but this did not matter in the long run since she was most likely to fail in this attempt anyway, as she had succeeded in failing in other ventures.

The unconscious fantasy here is that she is controlling the one that will punish her, by forcing the authority to repeat the role her mother had played throughout the long, symbiotic, early childhood period. She had discovered in grade school—as illustrated in the drawing episode—and most other situations after this, that she could act out the omnipotent fantasy by becoming the victim. She fully expected the analyst to repeat this pattern: to reason with her about the realistic danger of pregnancy, to caution her against taking unnecessary chances, to threaten her with rejection if she persisted in hurting herself. A great number of associations and dreams had made this expectation clear to the analyst who was on guard against the countertransference reaction at this moment.

What made this case particularly complicated was the still partially unresolved psychosexual identity, another aspect which frequently characterizes postadolescence, as suggested in the second chapter. The young woman had not reached genital primacy, did not enjoy penetration, and preferred clitoral orgasm by masturbation. The dream material contained frequent homosexual references. Her participation in sexual intercourse was mainly motivated by the superego aspect of her self-image, according to which a young woman should have sexual intercourse with a man so that she can consider herself a fully grown "normal" female.

In a classical analysis with a reasonably functioning adult, one would make interpretations that would produce memories, aiming at the furthering of the transference neurosis, until one would have connected the sources of the early ego fractures with the subsequent developments: the symbiotic tie and the illusion of love. In the analytic therapy of this young adult, one could not follow the same procedure, precisely because this is a postadolescent and this is not a classical, complete analysis. The present danger which the patient created as a resistance to remembering would have to be handled first or one may lose the chance of any modification, possibly even lose the patient. This may be another illustration of the variations in technique in post-adolescence, where interventions, which are not interpretations, may become necessary more often than in a straight analysis. The analyst in this case used the self-image motivation to cope with the victim role by suggesting that one of the many reasons why the patient may not be able to enjoy sexual relations was her latent fear of pregnancy. This was in part realistic, but far from an interpretation that could reach the deeper causes of her pathology. It was in part relying on transfer-ence authority—without however acting out the countertransference role—exploiting the transference by using the self-image to achieve realistic protection against further acting out. This is a detour from the main road of exploratory therapy, a temporary, but necessary disgression, which seems to be appropriate for some postadolescent patients. For the therapist it is an easy way out and, as we suggested earlier, sometimes comes to be used more and more frequently, until we have abandoned all exploration and are engaging in educational counseling.

In this case, for example, the young woman went to a birth-control clinic and protected herself against pregnancy, a necessary step against acting out the victim role, which however did not have any bearing on the psychosexual diffusion. The positive transference could be used in this case to achieve some insight into the etiology of the symbiotic mother-daughter relationship, by not reacting to the many provocations which the patient produced. Once she had fully discovered that it was she, herself, that had unconsciously arranged for the painful situations in which she found herself, the patient was able to inquire into the causes of this mechanism and brought new significant memories.

While the limited form of therapy was useful for a partial resolution of the end-of-role-playing syndrome, a partial resolution of the self-image dilemma and a considerable modification of all acting out, the psychosexual aspects of the identity diffusion seemed to require a full analysis, a few years later, with a complete transference neurosis and re-experiencing up to the second and third year.

It is of interest in this connection to note that when the patient returned for a full analysis, a few years later, she had succeeded suffi-ciently in her field of work to maintain herself but not to pay for analysis. In discussing this realistic problem prior to the analysis, the possibility of postponing payment until she could afford it was raised. However, the patient was by now too aware of the potential dependency acting-out and latent guilt to enter into this agreement. Instead she came back to a suggestion made by the analyst several years back, when she had been in twice-a-week therapy: to secure her legal financial rights, if necessary through the use of the law. Since this would have meant exposing some fraudulent use of her inheritance by her mother, she had hesitated to take this step until now, when it seemed possible and necessary. Apparently this step was no longer acting out of hostilities, but was taken in a factual, calm manner with the desired result and some improvement in the mother-daughter relationship, due to the respect the patient's mother felt for her daughter's forthright and non-punitive action.

With this as a basis the patient was able to finance her analysis on a somewhat reduced fee and develop a transference neurosis.

Although the analytic therapy which requires certain variations in technique has some definite limitations, it does not preclude the possibility of a full analysis later, either by the same or another analyst.

12. Styles of Free Association

THE LANGUAGE OF our patients is always of diagnostic interest, because the change in the manner of expression, rhetoric and rhythm of speech, variance in choice of certain words or repetition of others reflect varying ego states, and often are the first indicators of thinking disorders.

That patients ask for reassurance in their chain of associations is expected. How they ask for it should be distinguished. A patient may ask, "Do I make myself clear?" or he may ask "Does this sound reasonable?" or he may, after several attempts to express a feeling, add, "Did you get what I mean?" That obsessive patients take great pains in trying to find the right word is axiomatic; what words they reject or accept is of interest. Style of speech may change during an analysis as dream content does: use of concrete or abstract words, appropriateness of metaphors, use of symbolic language.

With the postadolescent patient we may get meaningful leads into the particular postadolescent characteristics in addition to the manifest and latent content by paying particular attention to their style of free association.

Certain *depersonalization* states as representative of identity diffusion can frequently be seen in young adults who not only have difficulty in beginning a sentence but whose ego fragmentation leads to trailing off toward the end of a statement, so that they usually do not finish a sentence. Their speech resembles a heavily revised or edited manuscript, where words are crossed out, replaced, written over, circled, and inserted above or below. This may be accompanied by low volume of voice and inappropriate hand movements, which bear no relevance to the content of the communication. They have of course been told about their manner of speaking by family, school, or friends and know the effect of their speech pattern, so that their use in therapy can be considered another tool in behalf of their resistances; however, the particular form it had taken over a period of years is of interest. It would seem that for the clinician the language, speech, and voice pattern may be studied by itself, instead of looking at it in a generalized way as a "resistance."

There will be variations in this pattern and degrees of unfinished or inaudible associations. Contrary to expectation, there does not seem to be any surface connection between the pattern and the content: the speech pattern is not directly related to a particularly embarrassing or difficult association. We probably should consider it a symptom and observe it the way we do any symptom: as a barometer of degrees of ego integration.

The pattern presents certain clinical problems since the unconscious purpose is in fact accomplished: we often do not understand what the patient is saying. In the beginning, when we have not yet understood this symptom sufficiently, some therapists will tell the patient that they had not been able to hear what he had been saying. We are, in fact, asking the patient to speak up. This kind of intervention may be used in behalf of the resistance (the patient feels that he was successful with his broken speech) or it may be used for acting out of the transference authority (the patient will apologize and for a few moments speak up and force himself to complete a sentence). A more clinically useful response would be to treat this kind of depersonalized speech as a fragment, similar to a dream fragment or a partial memory; that is, to identify with the patient and mentally fill in what he had not been able to complete with articulate words. This response is not possible for every clinician and at all times, since the broken speech is often experienced as hostility and reacted to with some degree of irritation.

The sophisticated young adult who has read about "free association" and comes to us with a set expectation of his behavior may cope with the depersonalization of speech by a number of reaction formations against the unacceptable broken-up sentence. One of the most common devices is the word-bridge, a frequent insertion of the word "and" between ends of half-sentences to give himself and us the impression that he is indeed "associating." The word-bridge is pronounced in a slow and drawn-out manner, to give himself time for a new thought or expression of feeling. While it is true that this is related to isolation —one of the common defenses—it is of interest also in the above-mentioned connection.

Another way in which young people tend to cope with the broken speech pattern is the run-on speech, comparable to run-on sentences, without commas, semicolons, or periods. Their pattern of association resembles an unbroken page of print, without paragraphs or interruptions. This method of flooding the therapist with words may or may not be a reaction against the broken speech pattern, but one may find a return to the unfinished sentence once one intervenes into the run-on speech.

Most typically, the voice and affect are flat in the monotone flooding; again, not directly related to the content of the material.

A very different style of speech may be observed when the post-adolescent struggles with the *end of role-playing* and demonstrates the variety of roles that he had been enacting in different language patterns. It would not be unusual to find quite different modes of speech in one session. The young adult may, for example, act out the role of the detached "intellectual" by interlacing every association with terms borrowed from his psychology classes or from popular reading on psychoanalysis. He will not say "mixed up" but "ambivalent"; instead of saying "angry," he will "feel hostile"; instead of telling us that he "forgot a dream," he will say that he "repressed" it. When a therapist comments on this defense, the patient may give it up and instead shift to the use of more weighty words in the description of everyday events. He will not have "bought" a magazine, but "purchased" it; instead of "thinking of" changing a course, he is "considering the possibility."

The same patient may, in the same hour, shift gears to the role of the member of his reference group and talk in "hip" language, which represents another role he has been playing and is considering giving up. If the therapist comments on the changed speech pattern, the patient will feel that he has been "put down" in addition to all the "bread" he is paying for this "scene." While he may have commented earlier on the complicated break-up with his girl friend in perhaps oversophisticated terms, he will now refer to this by saying that "Jane and I split." Two different roles, expressed in different languages, representing the ease with which he can shift from one to the other or, we may say, suggesting that he is not deeply involved in either role.

As for choices of clinical intervention, it would seem that the role diffusion would take precedence over deeper, instinctual conflicts. In terms of the young adult mentioned above, we would try to first understand the need for the shift in language before we could penetrate to the unconscious causes of his "splitting" with his girl friend, particularly since brief, intensive relationships had been a pattern with this patient. The change in style of his free association may give us the opportunity to observe a form of acting out of role-playing, which we had earlier referred to as a more primitive mode of attempted problem-solving. The language may be viewed as a form of externalization—as in all acting out—or as an attempt to extend the role-playing beyond its time. To the degree to which the postadolescent has come to an end of role-playing, the language shifts represent a transference resistance, which requires interpretation.

The *self-image crisis* is frequently made more transparent by the predominance of the superego or the ego-ideal in the young adult patient. This was illustrated through the speech behavior of a young man who would on occasion have difficulty in pronouncing words, regressing to a stammering pattern which had characterized a brief period prior to the beginning of adolescence. Although he had completely overcome this handicap, traces of it would occur either during some sessions or for a few consecutive hours during a week. This seemed at first related to aim-inhibited expressions, directly related to the latent content of the material. On further observation, however, it became clearer that the speech pattern was determined by the interference of the severe superego while there was no difficulty in associating freely, when the ego-ideal aspect of the self-image was predominant. It was of interest to note that when the superego was too prominent, the patient not only had difficulty speaking at all but there was also a difference in the choice of words. While he would usually speak in a light vein, using casual words and some humor, the language would become ponderous and heavy, the voice would tighten, the flow slow down to a near halt in speech.

At such times he would not report dreams freely from memory, but from a piece of paper on which he had noted it down upon awakening. There would then be few associations following the written report of the dream; instead there were long silences, with references to the piece of paper. On the other hand, when the ego-ideal aspect of the self-image was predominant, his memory was much less restricted, dreams and associations came easily and creatively, with no concern with order or logic.

The difference in the speech pattern can be better understood if one recalls that speech originally is set in motion, like any other organ function, "through aim-inhibited sexual strivings, desexualized libido and thus is the expression of sublimation which begins very early."[54]

Nunberg suggests in the same context that "if the speech-forming ego becomes flooded with libido; in other words, if the cerebral cortex or the speech apparatus (larynx, mouth) or both at the same time, become eroticized, a disturbance of the function of speech is the result. This disturbance is expressed in a regression of the ego, in relation to speech, to its magical phase of operation."

In the postadolescent phase of development, where the crisis of the self-image may be viewed as a conflict between supergo and differing ego-ideals, the disturbance of the function of speech is frequently represented in a stalemate, expressed in periods of silence. If the therapist should attempt to help the patient with this mode of silent communication by inquiring "what comes to mind," it is likely that he will get no reply, because the young adult is caught in the self-image predicament or, in instinctual terms, the ego is too damned up with libido to allow any free flow of speech. The chance for overcoming this handicap is better if the clinician addresses himself either to the ego-ideal ("you feel it best to cool it now?") or the superego ("shouldn't we see what is interfering now?") aspects of the patient's ego rather than to the total self, which at this moment is in a crisis. The open-ended question is likely to produce more anxiety or withdrawal at this point.

Another aspect of postadolescence which is often expressed in the style of free association is the *cognition of time continuity*. As with the alternation of speech behavior, observable in the end of role-playing and the self-image quandary, this characteristic too is visible in two contrasting manners of talking. After the cognition of time continuity had been repressed or denied for a period, this is then followed by a sharp awareness of the reality of time having passed, leading to a sudden anxiety in the speech pattern. The young adult quite suddenly finds himself flooded with a panic-like state which demands that he leave no moment unused in the session, but talk without interruption. He experiences the hour as a fifty-minute void which he must fill with his associations, speaking rapidly and, as one young adult expressed it, as if you are a sports announcer on the radio waiting for the athletes to appear in the ring and having to fill in empty time continuously. He may comment on his manner of speaking, by suggesting, with some sarcasm that he must not waste a minute, that time keeps on moving and every moment counts. One young adult used the latin "carpe diem" and the attendant philosophy to explain his anxiety.

This may be followed by periods of near lethargic speech or long, drawn-out interruptions and pauses, which are explained by the fact that there is plenty of time, that after all time is meaningless by itself or, as one witty student put it, time matters little "in the infinite scheme of things."

It is of interest to note that this vascillating attitude toward time, expressed in the style of speaking, seems to go parallel with the patients' use of time during the day or night. It ranges from a minimum of work to a very tight schedule in which every moment seems to count.

The clinical problem lies in the necessity of making a choice between accepting the particular language of many postadolescent patients or inquiring into some of the concepts, which frequently are shortcut expressions, as part of the style of speech belonging to one of the reference groups. The young adult, for example, who has identified with some of the currently popular "hip" groups and as part of this identification has adopted their language, assumes that we know that he means "money" when he speaks of "bread." While there is no clinical problem in learning the typical language of each patient, there is a problem when it comes to more than slang or occasional words, such as complex concepts expressed in shorthand abbreviations.

The young adult patient will tell us that her friend "turned her off," or she might say that he is "dragging her." These are two fairly typical expressions which are graphic and pert and can be understood in social conversation. However, as part of an association, we may have to understand more than the fact that the friend "turned her off." Is she repelled by him, quite suddenly, or as part of a development of their relationship; is she referring to a mood of an hour or a night; is she reacting to an impulse, to aspects of his character that she had not experienced before? In other words, we are dealing with the familiar problem of when to inquire into the patient's association, whether to ask for elaboration or choose instead to let the associations flow without our interruption. This is of course a basic problem of interpretation, which we shall discuss in the following chapter. However, in the case of some postadolescent patients, this is complicated by the consideration of his language. Do we use the patient's language for our inquiry: "What turned you off?" or do we rephrase it in more conventional language? The latter would require something resembling translation from a foreign language, including the difficulties inherent in rendering a word in different tongues. Should we say: "What upset you?" or "What repelled you suddenly?" Neither may represent the meaning of the words "turning off."

For another typical illustration, take a concept like "he dragged me." It can be understood to mean: "depressed" me, "bored" me, or as one patient explained, "made me feel like nothing." In other words, we don't know what the patient is saying, what feeling she is conveying with this shortcut expression.

In using the patient's slang for our inquiry, the young adult may feel that we are trespassing or "putting him down"; in rephrasing the lingo in conventional language, we may appear stuffy or "square." This is one dilemma. That we inquire altogether—whether in slang or non-slang—may well be used in behalf of the resistance by reacting to our lack of understanding of the language, rather than the underlying meaning. Not to inquire at all may also be considered as a sign of lack of interest on our part, since the sophisticated young adult is well aware of the fact that his language—like his long hair or dress—is meant to emphasize the difference between his group, his tradition, and the conventional world around him. Like the orthodox Jew, the anti-establishment young adult intends to emphasize his difference by a markedly different appearance and language. Young people look for reactions of surprise, indignation, envy, contempt—any number of reactions—except indifference. If we do not inquire into his language, do not react for clinical reasons, he will often feel that we are in fact hostile through our silence. While this is a common transference reaction in analytic patients, it takes on another dimension in this case where the language by itself would call for comment, aside from the meaning of the communication.

The silence of the patient, too, takes on another dimension with those young adults whose reference groups emphasize detachment, lack of reaction, and a minimum of communication. Where we tend to think of long silences as representing resistances in our patients, we probably will have to consider in some young adult patients the fact that by their standards of "cool" behavior, silence is the preferred form of "communication," as one young adult put it, citing as his authority the composer Cage, who wrote and performed compositions which consist of silence, or some avant-garde painters whose canvases consist of blank white spaces, described as "white on white."

No matter what the clinician's attitude toward these expressions of the current culture of young adults may be, they will have to be understood as part of the cultural background against which our young adult patients grew up. We could almost think of this milieu as an alien culture, almost comparable to a Japanese woman patient who would talk with more ease to us if she knew that we understood her culture, in which a girl was expected to walk—literally and symbolically—behind the man. We are used to adaptations to patients from foreign cultures, while we usually do not think of our young adult patients, born and raised in our country, as aliens. For some of them, the cultural differences almost amount to the same distance as with patients of different cultures. This will determine their way of speaking and make for a different style of free association than we are used to from our contemporary patients.

Just because we are concerned with safeguarding the classical content of analytic work, it is necessary to be particularly alert to the many ways in which the young adult reveals his complex personality in his communication with us. The matter of our reaction to this style of association will depend in part on our intuitive grasp of their messages, in part on the ability to handle them with tact and sensitivity. To remain aware of the young adult's style of association and to remain on sound clinical ground leads us to the discussion of styles of interpretation, the topic of the following chapter.

13. On Intervention and Interpretation

THE ESSENTIAL DIFFERENCE between variation and modification of analytic technique, between exploration and education, is the reliance on interpretation instead of manipulative intervention, on insight achieved through verbalization and working through, in favor of transference results or so-called corrective emotional experiences.

Applied to the characteristics of postadolescent patients with whom a full analytic experience is not always possible, this would mean a variation in the style of interpretations, without over-reliance on intellectualizations and suggestions.

To sharpen up this style of interpretation we should recall that even in the classical analysis, suggestions are used, which we label interventions (questions re: duration of a symptom, re: connection to the past). The difference between suggestions in analytic therapy and in educational manipulation seems to be this:

In a classical analysis suggestions are used as steps that eventually lead up to an interpretation; in the educational kind of therapy suggestions are used per se, as substitutes for interpretations. In the former, transference is used as a transmission belt that makes re-experiencing possible; in the latter, transference is used as a substitute for the original authority figures: we become the better parent, more objective, more loving, but still with the authority of "knowing better." Hence we speak in educational therapy of transference authority or transference results.

In the more limited form of analytic therapy, we would not use any more leading-up suggestions than in a full analytic experience. The difference would lie in the "depth" of interpretation.

The question of definition of "depth of interpretation" has been raised many times and probably not fully answered. However, previous discussions have helped us to become more aware of the complexity of the concept. As the research questionnaire reported by Glover[55] suggests, the concept of depth has been defined both in terms of degree of repression and inaccessibility to consciousness. The term has been used to connote either developmental levels or degrees of repression, and there seems to be agreement on the idea that "deep is a word that belongs in the first instance to the sphere of topographic description."

Altogether, the concept of depth suggests the older ideas of Ucs existing below the level of Pcs and Cs, as expressed by Freud in his classical iceberg metaphor.

As suggested in the introduction to the present volume, the shift from the topographic to the structural theory not only has given needed emphasis to maturation and developmental phases (such as post-adolescence) but it also has definite bearing on our therapeutic task, in particular our mode of interpretation. While in the topographic theory the purpose of interpretations had been to make the unconscious conscious, in the structural theory "conflicts over moral demands are accounted for in terms of the superego . . . it is important to make the patient conscious not only of the instinctual aspects of his conflicts but of their defensive and superego aspects as well, with careful attention to the content of anxieties involved."[56]

It is the superego aspect of the conflicts of our postadolescent patients that will be interpreted differently than with adult patients, because of the characteristics of this phase of growth which we had defined earlier.

The superego aspect of the neurotic conflicts of our postadolescent patients will require a less decisive interpretation than of our adult patients for two distinct reasons. First, because of the recognition that, for example, in regression we now recognize the temporary nature of both drive and ego regression, we are not as impressed with the "depth" of the regression as with the effect it may have on adaptation. Second, the superego aspects of the conflicts can not be as sharply isolated for an interpretation, because in postadolescence it is not always possible to distinguish between superego and ego-ideal, so that we can not be as definitive in our interpretations as we might be with patients whose self-image dilemma is less acute. This is further confirmed by Arlow and Brenner, who, in discussing regression, suggest that "transient ego regressions may be observed in both normal and pathological contexts. They form the basis of such phenomena as temporary disturbances in the sense of *identity,* transient episodes of *depersonalization* . . . and disturbances in the sense of *time* . . ."[2]—all characteristics of post-adolescence! It is axiomatic that such regressions occur in analytic therapy with many patients, while they still form a nucleus of what may be called a normal state of postadolescence.

It would follow that with postadolescent patients—with less well-established ego boundaries, the self-image dilemma, identity symptoms, end of role-playing, and time confusion—our interpretations would have to be more tentative than with adult patients. To some degree we will have to be as aware of the fluidity of ego states as with adolescent patients or borderline cases, although there will be periods where we seem to have achieved more stability of the boundaries and seem to be dealing with a sound ego core.

This is another special aspect of interpretations in postadolescent patients. Unlike the adult patient with a well developed neurotic core, with the young adult patient we do not always know what we are dealing with.

Where we have degrees of pathology in all the areas that constitute postadolescence, it is sometimes difficult to determine which area requires interpretation first. For example, a young graduate student, who had worked so brilliantly but erratically that he had been asked to drop out of the program of one of our most prominent universities, brought little material on his serious work interferences, but felt obsessively compelled to report his acute conflicts with two of his girl friends—while his lack of recognition of time continuity prevented him from being on time for his sessions—or for class—indeed, prevented him frequently from waking up in time for a ten o'clock morning session.

To get him to consider this aspect of his superego, ego-ideal conflict was difficult because it was not ego-syntonic and remained uncathected, in spite of the fact that he had to recognize the unreality of his frequently missed sessions. This recognition, however, was distorted by his identification with his current reference group in which "time" was considered as another pressure by the establishment to codify and organize life. To be free, according to this group, one did neither wear a watch, nor did one ever bother thinking of time, hours or days, but one remained concentrated on the inner "creative" self. It was, of course, understandable that this young man had a particularly rigid and successful father who was as precise with time as he was with money or verbal expressions. It is also significant, as an illustration of the economic bind, that this father at first refused to pay for his son's therapy because the choice of the analyst had been the young man's instead of the father's. The young adult, who had seen several therapists chosen by his father, determined to remain with the therapist of his choice and, instead of engaging in a futile battle with his father, asked for the cash value of his educational policy which was due at this time. He was now able to pay for his treatment, but considered the money his father's nevertheless. With this gambit he could further rationalize that the money wasted for missed sessions was not really his.

Clearly, for practical reasons, the matter of missed sessions, and sessions lasting twenty minutes had to be faced if the patient were to benefit from treatment. At the same time, interpretations that would make the therapist sound like father would obviously not be indicated. To strengthen the pseudo-ego-ideal by ignoring the issue would not help the ego to develop sounder boundaries, leading toward more realistic adaptation.

It appears that the transference was part of the postadolescent self-image crisis, requiring first a series of suggestions that would eventually lead to an interpretation which the patient's ego could tolerate.

With an adult patient who is firmly committed to a profession or a line of work that provides the means of paying for therapy, one might choose not to intervene in the superego conflict, expressed in frequently missed sessions, until the patient is ready to bring it up.

In the case of the young graduate student, the interpretation aimed at the superego conflict was prepared by a number of progressive suggestions, beginning with nothing more than a tilted head, a silent questioning of his routine apology for being late again. In subsequent sessions, when the patient repeated his "sorry I'm late" cliché, the therapist by not assuring him in the cliché manner led the young adult to the point where he himself noticed that he was being repetitious in both the fact of being quite late and sliding over it with the same phrase. Here the therapist nodded agreement, together with an accepting smile that encouraged the patient to dwell on the symptom a little longer than before.

For the first time the patient experienced and began to face up to the fact that there were forces inside his mind over which he had no control: he had reported how he had set two alarm clocks, used a telephone waking service, and put the clocks far away from his bed—all this after having gone to bed at a reasonable hour. In spite of his considerable intellectual knowledge of unconscious processes, this was the first time that he recognized the existence of the unconscious, of forces from the past which made him do things that he rationally had not willed.

At this point a careful interpretation aimed at the ego regression could be made, without involving the labile superego state, without aggravating the superego, ego-ideal dilemma, and without complicating the transference.

By interpreting the ego regression as a step backward to earlier stages of gratification, the superego guilt was neutralized or even reduced.

Educational suggestions, such as, "Something inside you didn't want to come here," would have bypassed the ego regression, activated the superego conflict, increased guilt, complicated the transference and countertransference.

That the ego-regression interpretation was of some therapeutic value was evidenced by the release of early memories: playing on the railroad tracks at four years of age without hearing the train and being rescued by older sister; jumping out of the family car before it had come to a complete stop—new material on impaired adaptation and reality testing as resulting from earlier ego fractures. The obvious masochistic component of the character structure was not highlighted at this point, since the patient was just now beginning to make contact with the concept of partial ego regression and its effect on his present-day life.

The shift from present to past to present, and the relative emphasis is another aspect of special interest in the interpretation of material when dealing with young adults. Because of the characteristics of this phase of growth, present-day manifestations or behavior will be avoided by the patient, while repeating already conscious memories is experienced as less painful. Since they can use the rationalization that in analysis one tries to remember, they feel at peace with their superego, while in reality the most difficult aspect of the analytic process is being avoided. The young adult, to whom we referred above, found it much more comfortable to dwell on the early memories—even discovering new ones—than to cope with the present-day difficulty of coming on time to his analysis or his classes in school.

This situation presents something of a dilemma for the clinician, who is inclined to regard recovery of forgotten memories as a greater therapeutic yield than the temporary, though necessary, modification of current symptoms which interfere with daily living. Probably with this more limited form of analytic therapy—both with adults and post-adolescents—some more time will have to be given to the ability to cope in the present with such elementary tasks as arriving for the therapeutic hour in reasonable time or attending classes in graduate school with a modicum of regularity. To accomplish this, without damaging the positive transference and without stirring up superego conflicts, is a particular challenge, typically in the opening phase of analytic therapy. Also, we do not want to create the impression that we are less interested in early memories and analysis of dreams than in the more mundane, practical daily chores of living.

Probably the guiding line will be the patient's ability to tolerate some of the anxiety that accompanies insights.

Greenacre,[56] Schur,[57] and Zetzel[58] have emphasized the connection between a patient's ability to bear anxiety and psychologic insight. Zetzel suggests that "limitations, inherent in the earlier developmental failure . . . influence the degree to which persons predisposed to great anxiety can respond successfully to traditional psychoanalytical technique . . . in the analysis of neurotic patients this capacity (to recognize and tolerate the existence of an internal, unconsciously determined danger situation) of achieving and tolerating the anxiety associated with insight is of decisive importance . . ."[58]

This highlights the topic of anxiety in analysis and in analytic therapy, and raises the technical problem of *reassurance,* as an intervention or one of the suggestive steps leading up to an interpretation. While there is agreement on the danger of rigidity in such modifying devices as reassurance, either for or against, the attitudes of analysts differs widely, depending on their theoretic position. As with the management of superego conflicts in postadolescence, the matter of reassurance too can not be left to chance in the hope that transference authority can accomplish what in the long run does require slow uncovering and interpretation.

Schmideberg commented on this particular aspect in an earlier paper,[59] when she suggested that "the fact that pseudo-analysts use reassurance instead of interpretation, or use it in a wrong way, should not prevent one from using it correctly, that is, combined with interpretation." She compared reassurance in analysis to narcosis in surgery, and most classical analysts seemed to be of the opinion that "while it might be a useful adjunct to interpretation, it could never be a substitute for it."[55]

With postadolescent patients in particular, the reassurance intervention will have to be guarded against having the opposite effect from the one desired: helping the patient to bear anxiety. For an illustration of an unwanted effect we might choose reassurance that sets off the conflict over time continuity. If we, for example, suggest that in time he may be less distressed about the failure of his examination or the loss of his girl friend, the patient may experience this not as reassurance but as a meaningless "putting off" statement, or as one young adult said in quoting a folk song: "work and pray, live on hay . . . you'll get pie in the sky when you die." This was his way of asserting that to him the moment mattered, while the concept "in time" was vague and amorphous, without reality and certainly not any comfort to him.

This kind of reassurance for him would increase, rather than decrease, anxiety, which would have been the purpose of the intervention, in order to prepare the ground for a lasting interpretation. We should think of the patient's ability to make use of the kind of reassurance that is ego-syntonic for him, rather than offer a generalized statement to which he may be allergic.

As with later interpretations, with reassurances too we might be on safer ground if we—at least in the beginning—do not venture into sensitive areas but offer simple and direct acceptance of a painful state, without attempting to redirect or ameliorate the feeling which the patient has shared with us. Unless we can have compassion for the way in which the patient has experienced frustration, we cannot console or reassure him, and would do better to remain silent, for nothing interferes with positive transference more than an insincere or casual attempt to reassure the patient.

To the extent to which such suggestions as reassurance and similar interventions are steps leading to interpretations, we should take care to plan each step as sensitively as possible, since this will have a definite effect on the impact of an interpretation. Conversely, we might say that ineffective reassurances tend to increase resistances, particularly with patients who suffer from mild paranoid thinking disorders, and specifically with young adults who are always ready to withdraw to earlier role-playing acting-out attempts.

The awareness of all the postadolescent characteristics may alert us to the many ways in which young adult patients may use our interpretations. While it is axiomatic that patients will at times "misunderstand" something we have said and report aspects of a session in slightly distorted form to friends, we can anticipate such defensive expressions with many of our young adult patients. We cannot completely avoid such distortions, but it is helpful if we hear what we say with the ear of the postadolescent. The question: How will this interpretation sound to the patient, how will it come across to him—with his particular characteristics, over and above the individual character structure— may make what we have to say more effective.

In the whole matter of language used for interpretation with our postadolescent patients, several exceptions to the common practices seem indicated. While it is generally assumed that we talk in plain, nontechnical language to our patients, there is a question whether we may increase or decrease resistance with the young adult if we "snub" him by not using the technical terms he is using. Partially as an expression of role-playing ("the good patient," the "intelligent young man"), partially as a result of the self-image crisis, many young adults tend to refer to their "superego," their "oedipus complex," or their "castration anxiety." If we asked them to spell out such terms some more, they will engage in an obsessional, hair-splitting definition bout, or they will fall silent, feeling that we are, as one patient put it, "pulling professional rank" or "putting him down." To substitute nontechnical descriptions ("your inner censor" for "superego") is likewise felt as editing or educational criticism. We do not want to introduce lingo in our sessions, but it may speed up matters if we, at least in the opening phase, accepted the patient's need to sound informed and go along with his use of technical language, without commenting.

Where we can make our insight felt is not so much in this aspect but in an insistence on not interpreting isolated words or actions, slips of the tongue, or any aspect of parapraxis. Whether the material comes from a dream or the report of realistic episodes, the young adult is often impressed with his "Freudian slips," his "interesting forgetting" of names or terms or similar isolated phenomena. Not taking up these fragments is both realistically reassuring ("I don't have to watch every word I'm saying here") and clinically sound, since we do not want to be sidetracked into archaic aspects but wait until we have a solid theme on which we can comment with meaning. Where the young adult needs to impress us with his intelligence, one can use this need to get him off the tendency to be merely clever. For example, when he reports a very confusing and disorganized dream, we can react by asking whether he can see any theme in this bewildering material. The primary value of such an intervention is to help the patient to get used to our method of tracing themes as a basis for any sound interpretation.

When it comes to the question of timing of interpretations, we may want to keep in mind the postadolescent characteristic of time continuity, which may make it necessary to begin interpretations earlier in the session and in the analysis than we might be used to doing with adult patients who can cope with the frustration of waiting, as a factor of time continuity, better than some of our postadolescents. This should not be read as meaning overtalkativeness in the analyst, but should be understood as another variation for this patient and this kind of analytic therapy. Short, compact interpretations that clearly hit the target and are based on sufficient data will usually be safer with the young adult than long and involved statements toward the end of the session or after several months of association.

Because the postadolescent tends to rely on his superego or his ego-ideals in coping with his resistances, he will often turn the analytic session into a learning situation and consider new intellectual knowledge as a sign of progress in treatment.

To cope with this defense, it seems particularly necessary to allow the postadolescent patient ample time for "working through." When Freud first used this concept, he said: "One must allow the patient time to become more conversant with the resistance . . . to *work through* it, to overcome it, by continuing, in defiance of it, the analytic work according to the fundamental rule of analysis . . ."[60] Since 1914, when this was written, a number of authors have stressed the parallel between mourning and working through, i.e., to correct faulty reality testing. There have been discussions about the necessity to treat "working through" as a special aspect of the therapeutic process or to consider it as part of the analysis of resistances, a viewpoint held by Fenichel,[61] or, later, Greenacre.[62]

In any case, the whole question of "working through" revolves around the effectiveness of insight, which has been described by Kris[63] as a circular process, involving the ego and the self-image. Applied to the self-image crisis of the postadolescent, we would expect recourse to the learning aspect of this process. The connection between affective experiences and learning theory, as emphasized by Novey,[64] suggests the temptation to fall back on passive wishes, which in turn will aid the resistance. For this reason alone, it would seem important with the young adult to wait with interventions or interpretations until he has reached the point where it becomes necessary for him to take the initiative and associate. This is one time where we cannot do anything but wait passively, instead of trying to interpret the silence or any other aspect of the resistance. As Stewart[65] suggested, the purpose of working through is not to accept the loss of a love object, as in mourning (passive), but to change the aims of the instinctual drives (active).

In reviewing the literature, Greenson arrived at a working definition of working through, by suggesting that "we do not regard the analytic work as working through before the patient has insight, only after. It is the goal of working through to make insight effective, i.e., to make significant and lasting changes in the patient."[66]

Another area in which the young adult's tendency to use intellectual defenses may interfere with therapy is in his understanding of free association. As a rule, when we suggest to the young adult patient to say whatever comes to his mind at the moment, he takes this as a request to verbalize his conscious thoughts. In fact, he explains his silences by saying, "I'm not thinking of anything." In other words, the emphasis is on thought, rather than on affect. We sometimes can help the patient with his stalemate by asking about his feelings at the moment, as he experiences them consciously. This inquiry by itself may startle the patient who is under the impression that he should tell us something "new," events in his life between the last session and this one, something he did or said—all expressed in the familiar statement: "Nothing happened." Inquiry into feelings or fantasies, daydreams or partial affects may remove some of the superego barriers which are used in behalf of the resistances.

While we can not use play techniques as is customary in child analysis, it seems obvious, as Glover suggests, "that at certain phases adult and child methods should overlap, so that the question of permitting or encouraging play activities in adult cases cannot be burked."[55] We are familiar with some play activity by our adult patients on the couch, who use their hands, objects in their pockets, a necklace or a thread from the dress or the couch for playing. Occasionally we may comment on such behavior, particularly when a patient quite unconsciously produces recognizable shapes out of a piece of tissue or twists his handkerchief into a rope. With the young adult, as with the child in analysis, we may prefer not to interpret such play behavior, because it will lead the postadolescent to more defensive, self-conscious attitudes. Certainly we would not want to interfere with such manifestations of the young adult's need to walk around or smoke, if this leads to more expression of affect, aside from the momentary value of relaxing tension.

Where depersonalization aspects of the identity diffusion lead to further difficulties in free associating, we may again vary our classical technique by taking a leaf from child analysis and ask direct questions, rather than wait passively for the patient to talk. Some young adults will tell you that they could talk easier if we asked them questions and, of course, this generalized request is a well-described form of resistance. While we do not want to help with the acting out of this defense, there will be occasions when a light inquiry into the manifest content may lead to a strengthening of the ego-syntonic forces, the ones that want to cooperate.

Where prolonged silences seem to distress the patient, enough reassurance is needed to avoid the increase of anxiety. However, this kind of resistance would require a transference interpretation, with full awareness of the negative countertransference which is often aroused by the passive aggression of the patient.

If the patient, after a long silence, suddenly comes up with a surprisingly sound interpretation, we may want to be particularly alert to our countertransference aggression. This kind of spontaneous insight with young adult patients, as with some schizoid patients, is not unusual and constitutes still another, often puzzling aspect of the variation in the style of interpretation with the postadolescent patient.

14. Special Technical Problems

THE INTERPLAY of metapsychologic and socio-economic factors which characterize postadolescence, frequently make for some distinct difficulties in treatment that we usually do not encounter in working with younger adolescents or with adults.

We are referring to a number of interferences that are not psychologic in origin, but often become serious challenges to both the patient and the clinician. We tend in our work to view most of the material presented by the patient as psychologic in nature, just as we tend to think of the patient-clinician relationship as a transference manifestation. However, not all of the patient's expressions need to be based on transference, just as some of the problems presented may be an expression of objective reality disturbances, rather than a result of intrapsychic forces.

For an illustration of a realistic interference in therapy of the postadolescent in particular, we may consider the issue of military training, which comes between the late teens and the early twenties, and while predictable, causes nevertheless a severe disturbance to the young adult, particularly when the country is involved in war. Not only is the patient at this point experiencing a profound disturbance in his personal life, his professional or vocational training, his relationship to those he loves, a reawakening of his identity crisis, and a heightening of all the postadolescent characteristics, but society now expects him to experience new emotions: patriotism, love of country, hate of an enemy he has never seen, identification with men he has never seen, a readiness to sacrifice his own life—a life which he has barely begun to fathom. The therapy which he has finally started, after a long period of doubt and hesitation, is suddenly interrupted when his local draft board calls him, and the young adult now expects his therapist to protect him from experiences for which he usually is not in the least ready.

This natural expectation produces a set of related problems specific to the situation: it changes the therapist-patient relationship and transforms the analyst into an ally, a benign friend who writes letters to official sources, describing details from the analytic experience which he ordinarily would not share with anybody. This is bound to affect

117

the transference and create in the patient feelings of gratitude and, later, guilt over his hostile feelings.

The extramural contact with official sources, draft board, government sources may at best postpone the interruption of treatment and give the young adult a deferred status. Many young people are concerned that this classification may interfere with future government or private employment. In many situations, letters from clinicians have been disregarded by selective service workers with the result that the patient's worst fears have been justified: his existing anxieties are heightened to a dangerous level, homosexual panic does set in in the case of certain patients, suicidal and homicidal tendencies have become sharpened, reality testing has been weakened. That this is of no value to society is understood; what concerns us specifically is the effect of being drafted on young adults who should continue to be in therapy until they are well enough to function.

That some young adults have sought such escapes as flight into foreign countries, attempting to live anonymously, or given up all attempts to adjust to reality is understandable for certain patients who are not equipped to make the necessary reality adaptations. Between the time the first threat occurs in the life of the young adult until the final decision of his draft board, many months, perhaps a year may pass. I have seen a number of patients regress sharply during this period with a reappearance of many symptoms. There have been more depressions, a return to hallucogenic experiences, a giving up of the struggle for success in work or study, a general loosening of controls. Therapy during such an interim waiting period is seriously hampered, because the reality threat is constantly hanging over any attempt to explore or reconstruct aspects of earlier ego fractures.

THE ANALYST IN DIFFERENT ROLES

In addition to these realistic environmental changes which affect the patient-therapist relationship during such a crisis, there is the constant danger of countertransference manifestations interfering with our work. Overidentification or counterhostility are both understandable reactions on the clinician's part, however slight or how well disguised. At the same time, the patient looks to us for constancy in behavior, as one of the few sane reality tests he has at this point of his life. That this situation demands more activity on our part—including the correspondence in our patients' behalf—than may be clinically indicated, is still another aspect of special problems in our work with young adults.

Not all of these special problems present as drastic a situation as the one described, although they too require a highly flexible and at times unconventional technique from the therapist. Most of the challenges arise from the particular position of postadolescents, in particular the overlapping of socio-economic and metapsychologic factors.

Because the young adult is no longer an adolescent, living with his family and yet not completely self-sufficient economically, all questions relating to his income, financial management, use of community resources, tend to come up in the analytic hour. There are times during the treatment process when the therapist will be called upon to function now as a social worker, then as a vocational guidance counselor, at times as a resource consultant.

Before we consider some of these specific situations, it might be well to recall once again that by taking over these roles even temporarily, we are using essentially nonanalytical devices and resort to the educational technique of exploiting the transference for reasons of expediency. That this will have an effect on the subsequent course of treatment, both transference and countertransference manifestations, is understood. As soon as we adopt policies of guidance, we are interfering with the transference, and for this reason alone, may want to weigh the current advantages of making a recommendation or offering a community resource, against the disadvantages of later interferences in our analytic goals.

For an illustration we may consider a gifted, attractive young woman who tended to act out impulsively, suggesting postponement of the end of role-playing throughout her adolescence and into postadolescence. This was observable in study, employment, and heterosexual relationships. When the previously described "escape into marriage" threatened both the continuation of therapy—her potential husband lived in Europe as his permanent residence—and the gains made in therapy, the analyst did act out some of his countertransference by implying that this marriage could not work for the patient and would, in fact, interfere with all her realistic goals. While he was careful not to make direct suggestions, his disapproval came clearly across to the patient, who correctly accused her therapist of acting like her father, even though she realized that he was more objective and thought only of her "own good."

There probably is no better evidence of the limitation of transference-authority results than this young woman, who fully cooperated with her therapist—and got married during his vacation!

DISRUPTIONS OF THERAPY

On the other side, there is the young adult from a rigid family who was so unable to handle his own finances—being careless as a sign of independence—that he was twice evicted and remained behind in his payments to his therapist for many months, without having made any arrangements for deferred payments. While the therapist had attempted to interfere with his patient's masochistic acting out through appropriate interpretations, it became apparent after a time that much more reconstruction and remembering would be necessary before the patient could cope with reality. In the meantime, the patient was about to be asked to leave school because of nonpayment of tuition and had been threatened with a lawsuit by a department store. At this point the analyst stepped out of his analytic role and functioned as a good social worker who helped his client with making a realistic budget, a totally new concept to the borderline patient. While the therapist was careful not to do more than was necessary for the young adult to experience the new idea of realistic planning of income and outgo over a period of time, he was, nevertheless, directing or guiding his patient. Since he kept such activities to a very minimum without elaborating on it, the temporary detour into counseling proved helpful. It was significant that the therapist did not continue with his patient's budget questions in following sessions, but made it clear that this had been, so to speak, an extracurricular activity which the young adult was perfectly capable of carrying on by himself. In other words, when the patient used this guidance activity in behalf of his resistances, bringing in more budget sheets, instead of free associating—the therapist checked himself and went on with the work of exploring, which they had undertaken to do together in the analytic process.

Altogether, the handling of money in the therapy of postadolescent patients tends to present a special problem of technique. With adolescent patients, where a member of the family pays the bill, money seldom comes up in the material of the adolescent, while in the case of adult patients, feelings about paying can be analyzed as part of the resistance. With young adults we have a mixed situation of part-paying by himself, part by a family member. This may be complicated when the parents have been divorced and perhaps both parents contribute toward the therapy, each with their own attitudes toward the son or daughter and the therapist. There are also many situations where young people experiment with employment, changing jobs and going through periods of unemployment. Most therapists who work with young adults are well acquainted with the sudden cutting off of funds by a family member, threatening the interruption of therapy.

When a young graduate student on a tuition scholarship discovered during the process of analytic exploration that he was not doing his best work because he clearly was in the wrong field, he took steps to change his professional plans, a step which caused serious financial repercussions from his family, who still partially supported him and his therapy. It was indeed the patient's superego, based on an identification with his strong father, that had made him choose a career which was not suited to him. In retaliation, the father, as part of his competition both with son and therapist, cut off funds, creating a typical special problem in the treatment of young adults: both the intersection of the self-image dilemma with the economic bind and the countertransference. As with any interference by the community, government, or family, the analytic situation is disrupted, demanding more active measures than may be called for by clinical necessity.

The punitive abandonment by father may increase all of the basic conflicts of the patient; in particular, it will heighten, rather than resolve, the self-image dilemma, the identity diffusion, and the hesitation to give up role-playing. For a period, withdrawal and mild depression may be expected, while the transference hangs in the balance. If the patient is to continue treatment, he will need the good will and trust of his therapist, a situation which has to have an effect on the self-image dilemma and his ability to associate freely in the future, particularly when he experiences both homosexual and hostile feelings.

The therapist, professionally obliged to continue with an ongoing case, is *nolens volens* put in the position of the "better father," a role he does not want to have in an analytic relationship.

There is the unrealistic possibility of interrupting or ending treatment, which will be experienced by the patient as abandonment by both father and therapist. It will undo many of the analytic gains, since such a solution will mean to him that the therapist was interested in him only as long as father paid for it, which makes father right and may tip the self-image dilemma in favor of the punitive, hostile superego—which had brought him into therapy in the first place, when he discovered that he had chosen the wrong professional career to please father.

In practice, the responsible clinician has hardly any other choice than to go on with the case and analyze his own resistances by himself, since this kind of situation will produce both aggressive countertransference and counterresistance feelings in the therapist.

USE OF TRANSFERENCE AUTHORITY

A different kind of characteristic young adult problem arises for the therapist and his analytic relationship to his patient when the post-adolescent, who has begun to set up his own home and style of life, inquires about community resources and wants reliable advice from his therapist for referral to a physician, a dentist, a gynecologist.

As in the analysis of adults, we want to examine all requests for advice as possible transference resistances, which aim to prevent production of memories by re-enacting childhood situations in the transference.

At the same time, we want to remember that requests for advice may also be based on ignorance or lack of experience in the adult world. There would be, for example, a considerable difference between a young woman patient who claims not to use birth control methods because "I don't know where to go," and the patient who is ready for it but has not had the opportunity to find a reliable gynecologist in this town to which she has only recently moved. Since she did not want to discuss this with her colleagues at school, with whom she was not on intimate terms, and did not know many people whose opinion she felt she could trust, the request for information from her analyst seemed to have a realistic basis. In other words, in the case of young adults, there may be reality justification for giving certain factual information, particularly about community resources. Both the insistence on analyzing every request of the patient and the eagerness to "steer" him to the best source may be an expression of anxiety on our part.

There are a great many small and large details of daily life with which he is not familiar, having been overprotected, or avoided the family as a natural source of information. Once our young adult patient is twenty-one, he is legally responsible for signing a lease, buying on installment, making verbal, binding working agreements. Because some young adults are notoriously inexperienced, they will at times be exploited by irresponsible businessmen—situations which, when multiplied, are bound to be harmful to their growing sense of independence and self-confidence. Again, as with other nonanalytic communications, we will have to guard against acting out the countertransference and become the better, protecting parent when we subtly suggest that the young adult call the housing department if the landlord refuses to return his rent deposit. This kind of casual advice or guidance will come up a good deal with young adults, and while we would not like to see our young adult patients hurt, due to lack of experience, we will have to consider the price we pay for this kind of friendly guidance in terms of the more basic goals of analytic therapy. It seems from experience by a number of clinicians who have worked with postadolescents that in the opening phase of therapy, suggestions will more seriously interfere with analytic work than during the middle or end phase, when there is emphasis on working through rather than uncovering and remembering.

This applies as well to the occasional acting out in postadolescence, particularly when it involves identification with reference groups who interfere with the analytic work. As with other interferences, we will be tempted to use guidance or authority to stem the tide of regressive, primary thinking and pleasure-principle behavior. This will occur after our more usual interventions have failed, due to either the stickiness of the patient's libido, or untimely, faulty interpretations. Just as we do not like to see a young adult make foolish, long-range commitments, we will regret his joining groups in which he takes LSD, gets involved in drug-pushing, or other illegal activities, or, as one group proposed, take the law in their own hands and steal what they desired from homes of wealthy acquaintances or relatives. Some clinicians, after having failed with both interpretations and suggestions, used authority by telling the young adult that unless he stopped this acting-out behavior, the therapist could not continue working with him. Another therapist threatened commitment to a psychotic ward after having told the patient that he was not capable of using good judgment by himself.

This is, of course, a long way from analytic therapy and possibly an acting out of unrecognized negative countertransference, which is just as damaging to treatment as any acting out in analytic therapy by the patient.

There may be, on rare occasions, room for the use of transference authority. However, as with suggestions or referrals to resources, this could not be effective until quite late in the treatment process, when we can be certain that disapproval will have an—even temporary—impact on the patient, and will be worth the price in increased resistance in the transference. Above all, we would have to be sure that the patient needs this kind of educational intervention.

For an illustration of this kind of use of authority, we would consider a young adult who, after several hundred hours of therapy, went into a slump and regressed markedly, using poor reality testing and increasing anxiety to a dangerous point. The material in the sessions at that time consisted of reporting his complex problems in graduate school, as well as in his place of employment. When the young adult mentioned that he had found a solution to his troubles by intending to sign a lease for a store with some unusual merchandise, instead of keeping his present job and continuing to study, the therapist detected a clear note of doubt in the voice of his patient and felt that the young adult, as he later admitted, "wanted to be talked out of this nonsense." The therapist used his authority at this crucial time to ask the patient not to sign any long-term store lease until he was quite clear what this would mean for his future in the long run. While it was made in the form of a strong suggestion, the clinician had been using transference authority, being convinced that this was a moment where he had no other choice. The indication for the use of this form of guidance came from the fact that the patient brought the material not in a regular session but by a phone call, explaining that if he signed the lease, it would have to be done before the next session.

Since the therapist well knew the forms that depersonalization episodes and identity diffusions took in this patient, he could afford to intervene promptly without marked damage to the later treatment relationship. That the young adult took the unusual step of calling by phone was his way of asking to be stopped from acting out.

In clinical terms, one might well raise the question whether or not the therapist's suggestion aided or hindered the resolution of the self-image dilemma: the patient was at this point struggling with the development of a more realistic ego-ideal, against the pseudo-ideal which had originally been promoted by his schizoid mother who exploited his narcissism and greatly increased his omnipotent fantasies.

To sign the store lease and "become rich quick" would have been acting out the pseudoideal. From all indications it seemed very unlikely that he could have financially survived or succeeded in this venture. Whether the economic failure would have strengthened his reality sense is a matter of speculation, since in fact he did not go through with his scheme. From all indications of the past history of this patient, it is quite possible that he would have learned nothing from a possible failure and financial loss, but would have blamed outside forces for his misfortune. At least this is how he rationalized his previous failures. The ability to learn from mistakes does depend on the capacity of the ego to critically examine one's actions without overreaction or rationalization. For this reason it seems likely that the therapist's protective guidance at this one moment bypassed the potential of economic upset and perhaps allowed the patient and his therapist to stay close to the significant core of the problem: the ego of the postadolescent, which is, after all, the final test of all our efforts.

15. Education for Analysis

THE CHANGE FROM the limited form of analytic therapy to a full classical analysis is a learning experience for both the young adult patient and his analyst. The difference was well described by a patient of European birth who likened the more protective form of analytic therapy to a skiing trip in the Alps with a group, while analysis to him was like a mountain climb with a guide who mostly is not visible. While you may be alone at times in skiing, he reflected, you always know that you can find your friends in a short time, but in real climbing all you have is the rope and you hope that the guide is up there looking out for you. Basically, you are on your own.

Aside from the increase of sessions, usually from two or three times a week to four weekly hours, there is the new adjustment to the couch, where the patient no longer has the opportunity to read his analyst's face for reactions or hints. The silence, which had been tolerated in sitting up, now is becoming ominous and at times frightening. The impulse to turn around and look at the therapist is ever present in the first period of this new adjustment. Since there is now nothing to look at but the ceiling, the patient hears more keenly, producing fantasies about the analyst moving in his chair, sounds in the waiting room, material about other patients or members of the analyst's family. Quite suddenly, for some patients, other fantasies emerge, stimulated by the new reclining position, the frustration of not being able to see the therapist, and the knowledge that the analyst has retained his sitting-up role and is able to observe the patient who now feels "more exposed" and "defenseless," as some patients have put it. The new material is frequently pregenital in nature, both surprising and embarrassing the patient.

For the analyst, the change from analytic therapy to a full analysis also requires some adjustments. If the patient has sharpened his hearing, so has the analyst, who, like the patient, can no longer read reactions from his patient's eyes or facial expressions. The rhythm of the patient's associations, the pattern of pauses or silences take on a new significance. Where the analyst may have been able to calm his patient with a friendly smile or a nod of the head, he now will have to put every communication into words, a change that requires keener awareness of his speech and the manner in which he puts an intervention or an interpretation.

The change in pace is often disconcerting to the patient who has been used to moving more briskly and making what he may have considered rapid progress. In reality, this illusion is the result of part transference cure, part unanalyzed resistances, which for a time leads to temporary modification of symptoms. The young adult who begins analysis will experience more frustration, because things move more slowly, since nothing is taken for granted, but everything is thoroughly analyzed.

For an example we may take a patient who had brought a dream during the analytic therapy to which he refers again in one of his analytic associations. In the original dream he had been concerned with his strange hesitation about looking at a movie of a prison riot—in particular his anxiety about the sight of men behind bars who were prying the steel loose with crowbars and had started to take guards as hostages. At the time of his dream report, his associations had led him to the wooden bars in front of his baby crib which had stood for five years in his parents' bedroom. He had been pleased in the original session that the dream and the associations had led him to what he had then termed "the primal scene."

The dream and the original associations came up once again during his analysis, when he reported intense feelings of hostility about a colleague. He said the man sitting next to his desk hemmed him in, kept him back, made him a "prisoner" to his old job—and from there to the old prison dream. He had no difficulties admitting his intense feelings of hostility against the rival on the job, nor considering the early feelings in the crib with the "bars," as a parallel to being hemmed in and prevented from moving freely. The resistance was expressed when the analyst recalled that the patient had termed the dream a "primal scene" expression and asked what came to mind at this session where he had recalled the earlier dream and connected the "primal scene" feelings with a current rivalry situation. Nothing seemed to come to mind but a sustained silence, followed by an angry outburst over the analyst's insisting on "rehashing old stuff that we have analyzed already."

This form of resistance is fairly typical in a young adult who has had some therapy and used the intellectual knowledge of "primal scene" to better defend against remembering and re-experiencing forbidden emotions from the oedipal period.

As in any complete analysis, the final determination of success is the degree to which the patient will be able to work through his resistances.

Some young adults who have had a less intensive form of therapy will be so resentful against the more demanding search of a classical analysis that they may ask for a return to the "easier" form of treatment. There may be requests for sitting up again, for coming less often, and for more response from the analyst.

It is a matter of judgment whether such returns to analytic therapy will be temporarily necessary or not, depending on our intimate knowledge of the patient's capacity to bear frustration. We are, as clinicians, confronted at such times with a dilemma of our own: to repeat the previous form of therapy may be increasing narcissistic libido and encouraging acting out; to insist on a continuation of the classical technique may produce such negative transferences that we may lose the patient.

Ordinarily, we determine in the initial consultation the patient's capacity to tolerate analytic exploration. In the case of most of our postadolescent patients, we apparently come to the decision to work with the more limited form of therapy that we have discussed before. During this process we may sometimes accomplish affective drainage of symptoms, significant modification of regressive tendencies, reduction of the archaic superego functions, no new transitory symptoms—in short, enough of ego-autonomy to consider a full-term analysis with the goal to resolve the most basic conflicts.

The decision to terminate psychotherapy and begin analysis is more difficult to make once we have embarked on treatment than in the beginning, when we were in a position to take stock of all the issues involved, as discussed in our chapter "Initial Consultation." One of the factors which contributes to this difficulty is our own narcissism, our investment in a case which has shown satisfactory results.

It is for this reason that some clinicians prefer to terminate psychotherapy patients and refer them to a colleague for a full analysis, in order to get a fresh, more objective assessment of the patient's capacity for tolerating analytic exploration. In any case, it would seem advisable to move very slowly from one experience into another, to share the potential hazards with the patient, and even to stress the difficulties, rather than make light of them.

We have of course a very different situation when we come to the decision, after initial consultations, to begin directly with a full-term analysis. As suggested earlier, this seems to be the case with only about ten per cent of the young adults who seek treatment. For these relatively intact young adults, some education for analysis also is indicated, although this will be a different kind of learning experience than for those postadolescents who have first been in therapy and later shifted to a full analysis.

The difference between the two groups is of course one of degree, so that we would expect to find the same postadolescent characteristics in both, in more or less pronounced form. Once we have come with the young adult patient to the decision to begin the analysis, we would start as in any adult analysis, by using the couch and introducing the basic rule as part of the opening phase. As in any adult analysis, we will get the beginning difficulties of lying down, the anxiety of talking to avoid affect, the attempt to control the analyst by silences or requests for help and declarations of being lost in this strange new experience. Teaching the young adult to work in analysis would consist in our selection of associations that represent superego expressions, typically projected on the analyst, as an attempt to avoid the self-image dilemma —a situation that we usually do not confront in an adult analysis, where we focus at first mainly on ego attitudes.

While we always aim in the opening phase at reducing the severities of the archaic superego, we have a particular situation with postadolescent analytic patients, since the superego versus ego-ideal conflict is more central than in adult patients. This is also one important reason why we would want to avoid at all costs to exacerbate the superego dominance. For example, to tell a young adult patient in analysis that his silence is a sign of "resistance" would create guilt and strengthen the superego, instead of neutralizing it sufficiently to expose the self-image dilemma clearly. Altogether, the use of technical terms sets up barriers between us and our patients, besides the fact that silence as a sign of resistance in analysis is so general that we are merely expressing a cliché. A reassuring acceptance of the silence, together with a first interpretation based on our knowledge of the patient's history from our initial consultation and our observation of his postural behavior on the couch, might yield more analytic gains.

With the young adult as an analytic patient we also want to be aware of the other characteristics of postadolescence that we had discussed in the first part of the book. It is, for example, not unusual to find that certain aspects of depersonalization as part of the identity diffusion become aggravated in the opening phase of an analysis. The shift from secondary to primary process thinking, assisted by the free association method, often leads young adults to feel that they are losing control and may, at moments, induce mild panic or, in certain cases, aggravate mild paranoid thinking.

Particularly where the identity diffusion is marked, we cannot afford to make deep interpretations, but need to give enough encouraging explanations to enable the patient to continue with spontaneous associations.

The result of early interpretations will be a flight into hostile panic and a possible negative transference development, which complicates the further work unnecessarily.

Because this is a young adult patient who is beset by not only his psychologic but also his particular sociologic problems, which we had discussed earlier, we will find woven throughout the analysis strands of material from the economic bind, the relationship to reference groups, and, on occasion, some of the special problems that we had developed in the previous chapter. While we cannot afford to go into these practical problems with the same thoroughness that we would have found appropriate in analytic therapy, we may also not be able to treat them as annoying interferences in our analytic work, lest we appear unconcerned or irritated by our patients' current difficulties.

As far as the patient is concerned at the time, these current economic and social interferences are more real and meaningful to him than his dreams and preconscious expressions of repressed states of the past. It is not unusual for postadolescent patients in analysis to combine the common isolation defense with the end of role-playing, one of the characteristics of this period. Being a patient then becomes another role, perhaps supported by his superego or his pseudo-ego-ideal, according to which he should be analyzed in order to be a "better person."

A young woman made this vivid when she referred to her dress as her "analysis dress," a dark, neutral-looking garment, which she wore only for her sessions. In her associations she referred to "making an entrance," "presenting material," "keeping you interested"—as though she were an actress, an entertainer, playing a role in a specially chosen costume. Dreams were "in technicolor" and had "good and bad guys," presented as though she were describing the scenario of a film.

Although the tendency to dramatize is a familiar defense from many adult patients, it takes on a special significance with the postadolescent who is struggling with the end of role-playing as one of the phase-specific characteristics. In the case of this young woman, role-playing had been her pattern in different relationships, different situations, such as school, job, social settings, and groups. She immediately took on the language and appearance of any new setting, acted and sounded like the person she associated with at the time—so that the neutral-looking "analysis dress" represented her image of the neutral, friendly analyst. Part of her education for analysis was the recognition that she was confusing roles—that it was not she who needed to be neutral, but the analyst. To begin to consider the fact that she had her own feelings, her own colors and style of life, independent from the object with whom she tried to merge, was one of her first surprising discoveries in the opening phase. Through a first clarification of the role-playing characteristic, this patient made contact with the identity diffusion and states of depersonalization as her introduction to the analytic process.

In a similar way, most of the other postadolescent characteristics need to be faced in the beginning as part of the preparation for the explora-tory work. This is true for the metapsychologic as well as for the sociopsychologic factors.

Reference had been made earlier in the book to a young man who was ready for a full-term analysis but did not want to either owe his analyst part of the fee or accept it from his family. He had preferred to come twice a week until he felt he could pay his way for a four-times-a-week intensive analytic experience. After eighteen months of therapy, he inherited some money from an aunt which enabled him to pay for an analysis. As he began working on the couch, he noticed an unusual resistance, difficulty in associating, and a brittle, annoyed tone in his voice. After the usual beginning problems had been checked out—the problems we have come to expect in shifting from one form of therapy to a more intensive one—it became clear that the young adult experi-enced a tremendous resentment against the large amount of money that now could not go for the things he had always dreamed of, but would go to the analyst. Because his family was not with him in his determination to have an analysis, he could not expect any further financial help from home, so that this small inheritance would be the last substantial amount of money he could expect from anybody. Since he was a graduate student with a scholarship and no certainty about his future earnings, it was understandable that the patient felt some-what deserted and completely alone. His panic-like fear of being desti-tute most of his life was now experienced in the form of massive hostil-ity against the analyst, the analytic process, and the function he would have to have in it: to come regularly and to learn to free associate. All of his postadolescent characteristics, both psychologic and sociologic, were aggravated together with his particular pathology: a thinking disorder with mild paranoid trends, lack of reality testing, and some hysterical somatic symptoms. The possibility of the personality disin-tegrating into a schizophrenic withdrawal was considered by the clinical psychologist who had administered the projective tests.

It would be realistic to say that in this case the economic bind of postadolescence triggered all of the other characteristics of this phase of growth and sharpened the existing pathology. While this sociologic phenomenon cannot be modified in an analytic relationship, free asso-ciation and intrapsychic exploration cannot proceed at an efficient rate unless the analyst fully acknowledges his young adult patient's feelings about social conditions that interfere with his growth. To maintain a neutral, passive position in the light of such material would most likely bring the analysis to a standstill. Ventilation of understandable, angry feelings about the economic bind, warm reassurance, and compassion would be a necessary part of the education for analysis in this situation.

It will also teach the patient that the analyst is not the all-powerful parent, a projection of the patient's omnipotence, but another citizen in a society where young people are kept out of the market, where there is economic discrimination against most postadolescents, where social groups are structured in such ways that they may interfere with the young adult's growth—a very imperfect society over which the analyst has no more control than his young adult patient. This aspect of education for analysis represents a first step into reality testing for the patient and a helpful reminder for the analyst of his limitations. Such reminders are not at all superfluous, since many of us tend to assume at times the Godlike role which our patients give us. In discussing psychoanalytic mythology, Glover suggests in this connection that "the figure of the 'perfectly analyzed analyst,' ready to cope with any emergency, for whom instruction in technical procedures would be superfluous, is an obvious derivative of the Myth of the Hero, a form of childish idealization that dies hard, not only among analytical students, but also among some qualified analysts, whose experience is lengthy rather than ripe."[55]

As far as the sociopsychologic characteristics of postadolescence are concerned, we should find no difficulty in fully comprehending the many strong emotions our young adult patients experience. While most of us had to recognize and learn to cope with these characteristics in our own postadolescence, "Civilization and its Discontents" will always be with us, so that it is only a matter of degree which separates our feelings about society and its contradictions from those of our young adult patients. If we let the young adult know that we are with him in the common struggle for a better world, we can better begin the analytic exploration, a process in which we often will have to be critical or noncommittal.

If the sociopsychologic factors of young adulthood have a more universal quality, the intensity of metapsychologic characteristics may be considered determinants for our decision on the most appropriate form of psychoanalytic therapy. The question: Can the young adult be analyzed? which we had asked in the introduction, may perhaps be answered again in a more qualified way at the end of the book:

1. When the postadolescent characteristics are all pronounced, the ego is fully engaged in attempting to cope with the self-image crisis, aspects of the identity diffusion, the end of role-playing, recognition of time continuity, and the search for the partner. In this situation, one would not want to strain the ego further by exploratory, uncovering

work, so that a full-term classical analysis would not be indicated, while a more limited form of analytic therapy has often proved possible.

2. When some of these characteristics have been modified and the ego has acquired the resiliency necessary for the strain of prolonged analytic work, a complete analysis has been possible in a comparatively small number of young people. Frequently it has been found useful to refer the patient to a colleague for the full analysis.

3. When the postadolescent characteristics appear to be negligible, i.e., when the young adult patient is relatively free from the phase-specific interferences, he would in effect no longer be a typical post-adolescent, but should be considered for a regular analysis with the same diagnostic criteria that we apply to all patients.

References

1. Spiegel, L. A.: Psychoanalytic theory of adolescents. In the Psychoanalytic Study of the Child, vol. VI. International Universities Press, N.Y., 1951, p. 380.

2. Arlow, J. A., and Brenner, Ch.: Psychoanalytic Concepts and the Structural Theory. International Universities Press, N.Y., 1964, pp. 28 and 81.

3. Hartman, H.: Comments on the psychoanalytic theory of the ego. In The Psychoanalytic Study of the Child, vol. 5. International Universities Press, N.Y., pp. 74–96.

4. Jacobson, E.: The Self and The Objectworld. International Universities Press, N.Y., 1964, p. 186.

5. Freud, S.: On narcissism: An introduction. (1914) Collected Papers, vol. IV. The Hogarth Press, London, 1951, p. 51.

6. Erikson, E.: Identification and the Life Cycle. International Universities Press, N.Y., 1959.

7. Jacobson, E.: The Self and the Object World. International Universities Press, N.Y., 1964.

8. Wheelis, A. B.: The Quest for Identity. N. N. Norton, N.Y., 1958.

9. Lynd, H. M.: On Shame and the Search for Identity. Harcourt, Brace, N.Y., 1958.

10. Mahler, M. S.: Problems of identity. Panel. J. Amer. Psychoanal. Ass. 6:131–142, 1958.

11. Greenacre, Ph.: Early physical determinants in the development of the sense of identity. J. Amer. Psychoanal. Ass. 6:612–627, 1958.

12. Glover, E.: Metapsychology or metaphysics. Psychoanal. Quart. May, 1966.

13. Jacobson, E.: Depersonalization. J. Amer. Psychoanal. Ass. 7:583, 1959.

14. Federn, E.: The ego as subject and object. In Ego Psychology and the Psychoses. Basic Books, N.Y., 1952, pp. 283–322.

15. Hinsie, L.: Psychiatric Dictionary. Oxford University Press, N.Y., 1940.

16. Freud, A.: Ego and the Mechanism of Defense. International Universities Press, N.Y., 1946, pp. 149–190.

17. Jones, E.: Female sexuality. In Papers on Psychoanalysis. Bailliere, Tindall & Cox, London, 1938.

18. Federn, P.: Ego as subject and object in narcissism. In Ego Psychology and the Psychoses. Basic Books, N.Y., 1952, pp. 309–14.

19. Sargent, H.: Quoted in Ekstein, R., and Friedman, S.: Acting out, play action, acting. p. 587, J. Amer. Psychoanal. Ass. 5:4, 1957.

20. Johnson, A. M., and Szurek, S. A.: The genesis of antisocial acting out in children and adults. Psychoanal. Quart., Vol. XXI, No. 3, 1952.

21. Bird, B.: A specific peculiarity of acting out. J. Amer. Psychoanal. Ass. 5:4, 1957.

22. Waelder, R.: Basic Theory of Psychoanalysis. International Universities Press, N.Y., 1960, p. 62.

23. Silberman, C. E.: Youth in the laborforce. Fortune Magazine, Vol. 71, March-April 1965, p. 130.

24. Mass youth unemployment. American Federationist. 72:8–15, May 1965.

25. Taylor, H.: The avalanche of youth into the laborforce. Monthly Labor Review. 88:544–546, May 1965.

26. Kent, S.: How to reach the college market. Printer's ink. May 17, 1963.

27. Malabre, Jr., A. L.: Focus on youth. Wall Street Journal. 164:1 & D31, 1964.

28. Cooley, C. H.: Social Organization. Charles Scribner's, N.Y., 1937.

29. Hollingshead, A. B.: Elmtown's Youth. John Wiley, N.Y., 1949.

30. Redl, F.: Group emotion and leadership. Psychiatry. 5:573–596, 1942.

31. Sherif, M.: Reference Groups. Aldino Publ. Co., Chicago, 1964.

32. Hare, A., Borgotta, E. F., and Bales, R. F. (Eds.): Small Groups. Alfred A. Knopf, N.Y., 1955.

33. Federn, P.: Healthy and pathological narcissism. In Ego Psychology and the Psychoses. Basic Books, N.Y., 1952.

34. Knight, R.: Borderline states. In Psychoanalytic Psychiatry and Psychology, vol. I. International Universities Press, N.Y., 1954.

35. Freud, S.: An Outline of Psychoanalysis. N. N. Norton, N.Y., 1949.

36. Jacobson, E.: The Self and the Object World. International Universities Press, N.Y., 1964, p. 187.

37. Hartman, H.: Ego Psychology and the Problem of Adaptation. International Universities Press, N.Y., 1958, p. 75.

38. Arendt, H.: Truth and politics. The New Yorker, February 25, 1967.

39. Farnsworth, D. L.: Psychiatry, Education and the Young Adult. C. C Thomas, Springfield, Ill., 1966.

40. Bellak, L., and Small, L.: Emergency Psychotherapy and Brief Psychotherapy. Grune & Stratton, N.Y., 1965.

41. Freud, A.: Introduction to the Technique of Child Analysis. Nervous and Mental Disease Publ. Co., 1929.

42. Monroe, R.: Schools of Analytic Thought. Dryden Press, N.Y., 1955.

43. Glover, E.: Technique of Psychoanalysis. International Universities Press, N.Y., 1955.

44. Menninger, K.: Theory of Psychoanalytic Technique. Basic Books, N.Y., 1958, p. 30.

45. Glover, E.: Technique of Psychoanalysis. New York Universities Press, N.Y., 1955.

46. Murphy, W. A.: A note on the significance of names. Psychoanal. Quart. Vol. XXVI, No. 1, 1957.

47. Saul, L. J.: The psychoanalytic diagnostic interview. Psychoanal. Quart. Vol. XXVI, No. 1, 1957.

48. Greenson, R., Lowenstein, R., et al.: Variations in psychoanalytic technique. Int. J. Psychoanal. Vol. XXXIX, March-April 1958, parts II–IV.

49. Freud, S.: Lines of Advance in Psychoanalytic Therapy. Standard Edition, vol. 17.

50. Eissler, K. R.: Remarks on some variations in psychoanalytic technique, Int. J. Psychoanal. Vol. XXXIX, March-April 1958, Parts II–IV.

51. Lewin, B., and Ross, H.: Psychoanalytic Education in the United States. Norton and Co., N.Y., 1960.

52. Racker, H.: The meaning and uses of countertransference. Psychoanal. Quart. Vol. XXVI, No. 3, 1957.

53. Berliner, B.: The role of object relations in moral masochism. Psychoanal. Quart. 27:38–56, 1958.

54. Nunberg, H.: Principles of Psychoanalysis. International Universities Press, N.Y., 1955, p. 122.

55. Glover, E.: The Technique of Psycho-Analysis. International Universities Press, N.Y., 1955. A Questionaire Research, p. 276.

56. Greenacre, Ph.: The predisposition to anxiety. *In* Trauma, Growth and Personality. N. N. Norton, N.Y., 1952.

57. Schur, M.: The ego and anxiety. *In* Drives, Affects and Behavior. International Universities Press, N.Y., 1953.

58. Zetzel, E.: Anxiety and the capacity to bear it, and Depression and the incapacity to bear it. *In* Drives, Affects and Behavior. International Universities Press, N.Y., 1949 and 1953.

59. Schmideberg, M.: Reassurance as a means of analytic technique. Int. J. Psychoanal. 16:307–24, 1935.

60. Freud, S.: Remembering, Repeating and Working Through. Standard Edition, 12, pp. 145–156.

61. Fenichel, O.: The Psychoanalytic Theory of Neuroses. Norton, N.Y., 1939.

62. Greenacre, Ph.: Re-evaluation of the process of working through. Int. J. Psychoanal. 37:439–444, 1956.

63. Kris, E.: On some vicissitudes of insight in psycho-analysis. Int. J. Psychoanal. 37:445–455, 1956.

64. Novey, S.: The principle of working through in psychoanalysis. J. Amer. Psychoanal. Ass. 10:658–676, 1962.

65. Stewart, W.: An inquiry into the concept of working through. J. Amer. Psychoanal. Ass. 11:474–499, 1963.

66. Greenson, R.: The problem of working through. *In* Schur, M. (Ed.): Drives, Affects, Behavior, vol. 2. International Universities Press, N.Y., 1965, pp. 277–313.

Index

THE LIFE